Philosophy for a Green Economic Future

Douglas E. Booth

Philosophy for a Green Economic Future
Published by Douglas E. Booth
Milwaukee, WI

ISBN-13: 978-1489538116
ISBN-10: 1489538119

Printed by CreateSpace

Table of Contents

Chapter 1: Introduction

The only philosophy worth thinking about is a "philosophy for the future." In the time given to us on this earth, how should we live and what should we do? This we have to decide. The future is all there is; the past is done and we can do nothing to change it; the present flits by as we stand around contemplating our fate. The past leaves an unavoidable deterministic legacy, but we aren't required to accept it in its entirety. We can't go back and change history and how it affects us, but we can alter our path as we move forward. Choosing what to do in life is our essential freedom, but just having this choice can be be overpowering and leave us frozen in anxiety. Are we truly condemned to be free, as Jean-Paul Sartre tells us? The idea of experiencing life, of having to decide how to live, as opposed to not existing at all, is both astonishing and deeply frightening. We can just trundle on and let the legacy of history and popular culture take us where they will; we can cave into the determinism of history and go with the flow. This is a choice. But we can also stand up and decide for ourselves what our future will be. Don't let your mistakes of the past overwhelm you; don't let the evil eye of others deter you from your chosen path. The future is your rose for the picking, but watch out for the thorns. Take lessons from history but don't let it rule your life. Strike out and take control.

These sentiments define the nature of the "existential" choice on how to lead our lives, one that inevitably involves us in a variety of either/or decisions, such as deciding to let others choose for us instead of doing it ourselves, or to seek material wealth as opposed to goals that bring meaning to life but not necessarily money for buying things. In recent history most citizens of affluent, industrialized countries have chosen a materialist path, and most spend the better part of their waking hours getting a living and spending it. The undeniable wonders of modern material progress endow us with comfortable, pleasurable, healthy, and interesting lives. Acquiring material possessions is fun, and in the process all of us together cause the economy tick along, creating employment and giving us all something to do.

While the immediate future will no doubt look much like the past, a slow but steady trend in human pursuits is taking us beyond a purely materialist existence. Even today not everyone follows strictly economic dreams. Some of us look outside of immediate possessive concerns to seek our meaning in life. Post-material pursuits take us beyond private hedonistic desires, such as the enjoying of a scoop of French vanilla ice cream, buying a new iPad, taking a vacation to the Caribbean, or wearing a brand new pair of soccer shoes to practice. What would a post-materialist do instead? A post-materialist soccer player would want to advance the quality of game itself (as a soccer referee might), or the success of a particular team (as a cooperating team member would), and would not solely focus on obtaining personal glory or the opportunity to wear fancy soccer clothing. Post-materialist soccer would be valued for its own sake, not just for the immediate private pleasure the playing of it brings. In a similar vein, one can value for its own sake photographing beautiful landscapes, writing about philosophy, advocating for gun rights, seeking governmental limits on climate change, researching the causes of cancer, fixing a clothes drier, putting a new roof on an older architecturally interesting house, creating a new microbrew, roasting a new variety of coffee, acting in a play by Oscar Wilde, or producing leafy green vegetables on Cairo, Egypt's rooftops to increase local family incomes, create green space in a city without much, and expand the supply of nutritional foods available to Cairenes.

To value post-materially is to possess a deep desire that some activity or being out in the world exists and flourishes into the future. True love is post-material and takes us outside strict self-concern, but pure lust is self-oriented and focuses on satisfying pleasurable desires.

There is nothing wrong with lust and pleasure, but we humans also express passionate attachments to activities and beings outside of our personal skins. Only in a state of non-possessive, other-orientation do we forget our ego and experience the wonders of the world as they stand for themselves. We can experience beings and objects as something over which we desire power and control, or we can appreciate them transcendently as free and independent with a path of their own in time, space, and the human mind. We can enjoy the continued existence of an ancient and beautiful musical instrument, such as a Stradivarius violin or a Guarneri cello, and the continued presence and performance of beautiful music that can be understood only in the human mind, and we can do this without personal possession or control. The same is the case for colorful wildflower-laden subalpine meadows, world series baseball games, great works of philosophy, well tended gardens, Shakespearian plays, French impressionist paintings, the architectural wonders of a Barcelona, the military precision of troops in formation led by the tunes of a marching band, jazz performances in the bars of New Orleans, or a stable climate free of greenhouse gas perils.

For post-materialists, experiences stand above consumer possessions in importance. Possessions are necessary to life, but it's experiences that count for life's greatest satisfactions. Post-materialism takes us beyond our strictly personal interests toward a more open and less self-conscious connection with the larger world. We will always worry about our own, private well-being, but our new-found post-materialist values can move us to look outward beyond our personal skin toward the amazements of existence as such. The idea of experiencing life, as opposed to not existing at all, is both astonishing and deeply frightening as already noted, but can foster in us a sense of wonder and cause us to engage in care for all that we love, and, in particular for the Earth itself, the source of our being.

All this sounds great, even utopian, as an offering of a better future for anyone disenchanted with modern life, but I am getting ahead of myself. Post-materialism as a trend has only just begun with barely perceptible baby-steps. None of us will become full-fledged post-materialists overnight. We need to understand the importance of our materialist ways first, and then we can look into the meaning and nature of slowly rising and not much noticed post-materialist practices in the midst of our material affluence. What we will see in this exercise is that philosophy truly matters. If our philosophical values slowly but inexorably change over time, the way we live, and the impact we have on the world around us, will also change. By looking at trends in the values we possess, we can gain insights into the direction we are headed. In these pages, our concern will be directed especially to the values we hold toward our natural environment, and in particular toward the global problem of climatic warming. Philosophy can in this way tell us not just about how we should live, but about how the future may unfold for us and the natural world from which we gain sustenance and much of our spiritual inspiration. But first we need to understand how our values of the past have shaped where we have been. The past can't be altered, but we need to know the nature of our point of departure as we head into the future.

Chapter 2: Meaning, Materialism, and the Suburban Dream

The quest by philosophers for a singular and final explanation of the meaning of life has been largely given up as a fruitless exercise. Instead, we are left to deal with this task on our own. Most of us say that we believe in God, and that religion takes care of all questions of ultimate meaning. The trouble with this kind of response for us Americans is that we pay lip service to religion, but then what we really do is go to the mall. We are materialists, body and soul, through and through, and we live accordingly. We find our meaning not in the heavens, but in goods. As materialists we believe that the essential purpose in life is to gain access to financial resources and to use them to acquire material possessions. Accomplishing this purpose is our passion. Our temples are the Mall of America and Amazon.com. Meaning comes from adopting purposes and values about which we care passionately and pursuing them through actions in the world, and the predominant form of meaning today is deeply materialist.

Our dream of where to live for over a century in this country has been fundamentally suburban; the city doesn't suit our consumerist ways as well and conveniently as the suburbs. Fifth Avenue in New York and the Magnificent Mile in Chicago have consumer palaces we love to visit, but most of us can't afford to buy much in these places. Our real consumer paradise is in the suburban malls and big box stores where we can find an abundance of treasures we can actually afford, and where we can drive right up and walk right in to buy what our heart desires. We can't afford the big city cathedrals of luxury retailing for the elite, but we are blessed with the affordable and accessible big box suburban churches of consumption for the middle class.

You might think I am out to ridicule the vast majority of Americans who enjoy the delights of accumulating consumer possessions, but this would not be too smart given the current predominance of materialist sentiments. Instead I will begin by reinforcing the significance and importance of the suburban consumption machine and those who drive it. By-and-large, despite what many academics say, suburban dwellers are happy people, and they want to stay that way. They choose the suburbs for good reason; this is where they can most fully realize their material dreams. Most importantly, these are the people that keep the economy humming, and when they face unemployment, declining housing values, and foreclosures, the economy as a whole suffers. Lets take a quick look at what survey researchers have found out about materialism and reported life satisfaction.

***

Many happiness researchers postulate that materialists will be less satisfied than others because they are caught up on an economic treadmill that requires increasing amounts of time earning and buying in order to sustain the delights of consumption. Life on this treadmill sacrifices a deeper happiness that comes from having time to engage fully in a variety of satisfying pursuits: interacting with family and friends; involvement in community activities, such as amateur sports, charitable causes, politics, or church; putting energy into some activity so engaging as to cause one to lose all sense of self-consciousness; or accomplishing some purpose that expresses one's deepest commitment to highly regarded personal values.[1] The losing of self-consciousness through intense engagement psychologists refer to as flow, and a wide variety of activities can produce it—pitching in an a highly competitive baseball game, writing important software code, working on a painting of a desert landscape at sunset, pursuing a deer with a bow and arrow, or climbing a fourteener, such as San Luis Peak in Colorado. The same is true of accomplishing a valued purpose such as writing a book about how to bring climate change to a halt, successfully helping elect a candidate for political office who will support cap and trade, or completing a lay sermon about belief in God before a Unitarian church congregation.[2]

Survey research has indeed confirmed that materialists do experience less life satisfaction than others, primarily because they spend less time with their families and more on economic pursuits.[3] But recent findings paint a more nuanced picture of the relationship between materialism and happiness. In college, the more materialistic students tend to be more outgoing and popular, less accomplished academically, and more likely to take up majors with the best income earning prospects, such as business and engineering, than their less materialistic counterparts. After college, many, but not all, materialistically oriented graduates achieve financial success. Those that do turn out to be just as satisfied with their lives as their peers who care less about making money, but those who aspire to financial accomplishment and fail to achieve it experience a small but statistically significantly lower level of life satisfaction than others, again because of less time spent with family. Actual economic success in effect compensates for lost satisfaction from extra time on an economic treadmill, but if you jump on the treadmill and fail to advance, your happiness suffers. In sum, materialistic suburbanites who achieve economic success appear to be as happy as anyone else, and those who fail suffer for it, but not by much.[4]

***

An entertaining writer skilled at explaining how we extract meaning from materialism is James Twitchell. Consider the quote that begins the final chapter of his book, *Lead Us Into Temptation: The Triumph of American Materialism*.[5] Here it is:

> Sell them their dreams. Sell them what they longed for and hoped for and almost despaired of having. Sell them hats by splashing sunlight across them. Sell them dreams—dreams of country clubs and proms and visions of what might happen if only. After all, people don't buy things to have things. They buy things to work

for them. They buy hope—hope of what your merchandise will do for them. Sell them this hope and you won't have to worry about selling them goods.

These are the words of Helen Landon Cass, a female radio announcer, spoken before a convention of salesman in 1923. Is American materialism indeed the answer to the quest for meaning in life? Cass seems to think so and so does Twitchell. Anyone concerned with economics and the pursuit of meaning can't ignore what Cass and Twitchell have to say given the extraordinary role of consumer desire in our global economic reality today. How could acquiring possessions be an act of self-creation that defines what we care about in the world? What exactly is the power of stuff? Let's see what Mr. Twitchell has to tell us about consumer desire and meaning. But first, my personal story of seeking meaning through consumption.

I love to spend a few weeks each winter hiking and backpacking in the Sonoran and Mohave Deserts and a month or so in the summer doing the same in the high-mountain Colorado Rockies. I spend a lot of time dreaming about this when I am not actually doing it. I see myself as a botanizer and photographer of wildflowers and landscapes in deserts and high mountain meadows of stunning natural beauty. To do this I need equipment and I need to get there. Navigating the desert or getting up rough mountain roads to trailheads is eased with a four wheel drive vehicle, and now that I am officially old, what could be better than a Toyota RAV4. This I have come to describe as my mountain camping car, partly to assuage my guilt over owning a vehicle that gets only pretty good mileage. You might think that I bought this car to project a certain public image, but I have since determined I did it as a matter of self-definition. Driving it around makes me feel like the hiker and backpacker I am any time of year. A piece of my self-creation is what I drive, but in my own eyes, not so much the eyes of others. I now discovered that most drivers of a RAV4 use it more for going to the mall, judging from their body shapes, than driving up mountains to trailheads. Owning such a car for me symbolizes my freedom to explore and have adventures, something that I doubt others perceive. There is lots of other little self-expressive things I buy that has little to do with my public image. I love the small, lightweight stuff that eases the task of backpacking like little stoves, little tents, lightweight sleeping bags, and so on. This is an REI-based (the premier outdoor store and cooperative) consumerism that helps to define who I am. I have just recently, for example, discovered moisture-wicking t-shirts which I just love. For a while, I put my consumer effort into having car camping comfort goods such as a larger tent, chairs, and a screened porch around the picnic table, all of which I have come to enjoy in my old age. I have even looked at some of the smaller travel trailers, but, like Diderot's robe, buying one would lead to still other needs, like a bigger, more powerful car.

Recently, I have experienced a modest transformation in my attitude toward all this. I still absolutely love the idea of high mountain exploration even though I am slowing down in my dotage, but I now see car ownership as a pain and driving on four wheel drive roads as creating more anxiety than pleasure. My RAV4 has been sold to my son, a big guy that has to squeeze to get into smaller vehicles and at 26 has yet to own a car (he needs it more than I), and my wife and I will get along on just one car, a well-worn Toyota Corolla. To get to the mountains I will rent something, and I am scaling my car camping back to mostly backpacking sized equipment that will fit on a plane. I would like to get a new camera though with a larger image sensor and a good macro lens for wildflower photography. There is always something more to buy. In any case, self-creation and the search for meaning is a dynamic process, and the REIs of the world do a great job selling me objects of my dreams.

Academics jump on commercial consumerism as a mindless popular caving into Madison Avenue psychological manipulation motivated by a corporate conspiracy to maximize business profits. A mass production economy, capable of creating through the magic of advanced technology a cornucopia of material goods, requires for survival a mass consumption economy able to absorb all that is produced. Inadequate demand would doom such an economy to stagnation and depression. To prevent this, goods must do more than just stimulate people to consume beyond basic need. To transform the ordinary into objects of desire, the practice of marketing adds meaning, through advertising, packaging, branding, and fashion, to products that inherently lack it. When we buy goods, we gain not just something that is materially functional, but something that gives spark and significance to our lives. "And what could ever be wrong with that?", Twitchell rhetorically asks of us. What exactly is the problem with creating self-identity and expressing what's especially important to us through the brands of goods we voluntarily choose to possess? Isn't true democracy the right to choose whatever we want to consume absent substantial harm to others?

In order for goods to express something beyond their physical being, they must possess an identifiable brand to which a meaning can be attached. An ad at the bottom of the *New York Times* business page caught my eye recently (April 13, 2011) as expressing visually and in text a number of ideas to connect with a particular brand. Pictured in the ad is Breitling's Superocean watch at $3,335 along with a picture of a diver poking his shaved head in swimming goggles above water with the nearby text, "Herbert Nitsch, Airline Pilot, Deepsea Diver, Extreme Record Breaker." The diver and the watch standout in stark contrast against a dramatic black background. The implication to me is that people who are athletic, accomplished, powerful, heroic, affluent, and discerning in their tastes own such luxuries as Superocean underwater watches. Advertisements cannot be overly complicated or they fail in their task to attract viewers and potential customers. Very quickly we learn in this ad that someone with heroic qualities endorses the product. If we aspire to the values and virtues expressed in the ad, then we might well give serious consideration to purchasing the watch depicted, if we can afford it and even if we never go diving. If we acquire the watch, then we in effect endorse what it symbolizes as expressed in the ad, not only for our own sake, but for the sake of admiring others who know about Breitling which supplies "instruments for professionals," as the ad tells us. A life of meaning for most of us amounts to choosing our heroes, and advertising endorsements facilitate this task.

As Twitchell would no doubt argue, advertising adds a meaning to goods that they intrinsically lack. Look at any advertisement, and I am sure you can discern the intended message conveyed about virtues of the brand and the people who consume it. Advertising and branding together take over from religion much of the means for satisfying our hopes. Prayer to gods as the path to getting what we want out of life gets displaced in the world of commerce by the magical power of goods. Nothing is more magical to me than my Ipod Touch which connects me to the world, whenever wifi is in range, and allows me to socially connect with everyone I know with a touch of the screen. It also permits me to record my thoughts and ideas when I am relaxing in a Rocky Mountain meadow campsite far from civilization, and even read a book, as long as my battery lasts. I can imagine how much more magical an Ipad would feel. It's not just advertising in a world of high technology that gives a product meaning, but the design details as well. We want an Ipad not just because of its attractive ads, but to experience all the wonderful things it can do for us. Just like prayer, commerce will get you to heaven, only it will be a heaven on earth.

One might think that a mass production economy and its capacity to produce cheaply huge numbers of identical goods would lead to us all consuming the same things and in the process creating highly similar personal identities. Through the wonders of competition in advertising, branding, product design, packaging, and fashion, diversity prevails in the consumer world. Go to any mall, or cruise the internet, and you will discover a never-ending panoply of goods. We all have plenty to choose from in creating our own special form of life. Branding seems to refute the notion of consumer individuality since many of us select the same identical product. If enough of us didn't for a given brand, it wouldn't survive. Consuming a particular brand isn't a creative act so much as selecting a combination of brands to consume. Through choosing an ever-changing combination of brands we continuously seek identity and self-creative meaning. We brand ourselves and construct a coherent self-image by consuming a constellation of products. Life must cohere as Diderot found out in the purchase of his new robe. For those of you who don't know the story, Diderot lived a messy life including the wearing of a robe that was little more than a rag, which he decided was just too much. He thus acquired a rather plush new one that made the rest of his surroundings look even more tawdry. Soon he bought entirely new furnishings to match his new robe. In the consumer world, buying one thing inevitably leads to another. Diderot in modern terminology branded himself by creating a coherent fashion. How do we today learn about this process? Twitchell tells us it's TV that does the job, but I suspect that currently its more than that, given the rising use of the Internet, especially by the young.

In the end, what different types of branded products do for us is what matters. Some of what products achieve is magical, yet mundanely functional. Advil gets rid of our aches and pains, Tide gets our cloths clean, Cheerios keep our heart in shape, and Coke tastes good. We feel more sensual with exotic perfume or aftershave on, and as a result we probably behave more sensually and increase our attractiveness to others. An expensive watch communicates our wealth and power in society. Fancy cars do the same while also giving us an environment of comfort and luxury and a powerful machine that can go from 0 to 60 in nothing flat. Both watches and cars rise to the status of works of art, as can a tastefully appointed living room, or a diamond bracelet. A Green Bay Packer sweatshirt in Wisconsin expresses an affiliation that connects one socially to numerous others. A Northface jacket symbolizes the outdoor activity the wearer presumably undertakes. Goods are, and always have been, signals and signs to others as well as ourselves about who we are, what we believe, and what brings meaning in our lives. Above all, goods communicate. So how does this all related to the way we choose to arrange ourselves in space?

***

At the mid-Twentieth Century, middle-class Americans everywhere turned their backs on the old, established central cities as places to live, and they did this for good reasons. Streets were traffic-clogged, city governments were often corrupt, crime was fearsome, the quality of schools was in decline, the air was often polluted, the streets were noisy, housing was densely packed and overcrowded, and low-income immigrants of a different race were arriving daily. By contrast the suburbs looked like a dream—open green spaces, new, detached single family houses that one could own, local control of government, social and racial homogeneity, and the ability to commute to work in the privacy of one's car. What could be better?

Before World War II, cities retained the hub-and-spoke shape and relatively high density given them by the electric trolley. People either walked to work or they rode the trolley, and many lived compactly in apartments or other kinds of multifamily housing. Outward spreading of the relatively well off to new "streetcar suburbs" for single-family housing occurred in all large cities, but population densities stayed relatively high. The economic and cultural heart and soul of the city remained at its center, but all this was about to change.[6]

Americans could have followed the prewar approach of basing the shape of urban space on public mass transit and compact housing, but they chose a distinctly different path—the creation of an urban transportation system and access to suburban housing rooted in a love affair with the automobile. A majority of urban Americans now live in suburbs instead of central cities and reside in locally governed, low-density municipalities and commute from detached single family homes to low rise business and commercial buildings surrounded by convenient parking. In the process, most Americans now avoid ever setting foot in a high-density central city. Not only did people move to the suburbs, but along with them so have businesses. The multistory central city factory located on a rail line or near a dock found itself replaced by a low-rise suburban plant with its truck bays and close access to freeways. Densely packed older department stores and high-rise offices in the central city business district have been out-competed by low-rise suburban shopping malls and office parks with their ample parking and close proximity to housing developments. Only in the suburbs could our new postwar consumer dream of possessing spacious, well appointed single-family dwellings and sleek, powerful motor vehicles be easily satisfied. Nothing is more important in symbolizing our material accomplishments than our homes and our cars. We fill our living spaces with those consumer items that define who we are, and choose motor vehicles that reflect our deepest values in life. In the U.S., what matters most is where one lives and what one drives. Governments at all levels supported and fostered this dream with home loans guaranteed against default, tax deductions for mortgage interest payments, and massive systems of freeways and highways that eased the task of moving around the suburban landscape.

For several decades following World War II, suburban expansion and the industries it fueled pumped up consumer and investment spending and assured national economic prosperity. In the U.S., the passion for financial accomplishment and material goods has taken a distinctly and even radically suburban form. In our present economic crisis, the suburban dream faces serious challenges from the current middle class experience of rising housing foreclosures, high unemployment rates, and above normal prices at the gas pump. Our economy seriously needs a new engine of growth. The question we now want to address is whether a shift in attitudes and values is in the cards that will in itself push us toward an economy rooted in a less materialistic, more compact and environmentally friendly form of living.

Now that you are fully aware of something you no doubt already know about and experience around you on a daily basis—the nature of materialism—we can move along to describe what appears to be a new philosophy for the future, post-materialism, something probably less familiar to you, although if you are reading this, chances are you are a part of the trend.

Chapter 3: Post-material Values and a Philosophy for the Future

The Google founders, Sergey Brin and Larry Page, started out to create the best Internet search engine there is, not to make a ton of money. It took a while for them to accept the idea of ads related to searches as the path to generating revenue. The usual web ads that obnoxiously flash at you or fill up your screen Brin hated. Brin and Page instead happened on the brilliant idea of simple, unobtrusive text ads which turned out to be a gold mine. Simplicity, speed, and efficiency is what Brin and Page were after, not the money. They didn't like org-chart modes of business organization and chose a flatter more decentralized and chaotic form, but it worked. Informal meetings and intense, competitive recreation along with free food kept the place running. Brin didn't like marketing and wanted to use the marketing budget at one point to inoculate Chechen refugees against cholera because it would be a good thing to do and could bring attention to Google. Google's well-known guiding moral standard is "don't be evil." On the job physical activity energizes life at Google—pool, ping pong, and, of course, roller hockey, the one most encouraged by Brin and Page. The original workspaces were filled with crash cots, funky second hand furniture, makeshift room dividers, exercise balls, and ever-present white boards for scribbling down the next big ideas. The annual ski trips for Googlers (i.e. Google employees) were legendary for their decompressing party atmosphere. Google is an offbeat place to work like no other, but to become a Googler means working long hours with others in small groups, accepting meritocratic values, and being assertive, creative, a risk taker, and playful. Constant anxiety about measuring up comes with the Googler territory.[7]

In the world of high tech, it's not your ethnic origin and social background that matters. It's the software code you have written lately or the successful new application or popular new gadget you have helped to create that confers status. Young techies are a tolerant lot; they judge according to merit and accomplishment, not according to appearance or skin color, and they delight in a wide range of behavior patterns and personal styles. Tattoos and body piercing jewelry are fine as well as unusual tastes in music, art, or sexual practices. The experience of life matters, not where one comes from or what one owns.

The high tech world, despite its incredible financial success, embodies a modest beginning of a movement away from purely materialist concerns toward post-materialistic personal self-expression, social tolerance, and interesting life experiences. Seeking meaning in life boils down to adopting and pursuing purposes about which one cares passionately. If we have strong materialist inclinations, then we will find meaning predominantly in the economic arena where we will pursue wealth and material possessions. If we follow a post-materialist path, our actions in the world will take us beyond strictly economic pursuits. If you did nothing but look to advertising and the popular media, you might think that post-materialism is a utopian dream, but social scientists over the past several decades have detected a modest but persistent shift favoring values that take us beyond a predominant desire for wealth and consumption.

I don't want to force you through a tedious, article-by-article, academic-style summary of the research to prove that post-materialism is indeed a significant trend that will take us into a new and different future, but I do want to give you a flavor of what the post-materialist idea is all about. What I am going summarize for you now is not philosophical speculation, but actual, real world research findings on human attitudes and belief. Before I do this, I want to acknowledge the one researcher responsible more than any other for discovering the post-materialist trend, University of Michigan professor, Ronald Inglehart, whose findings in the 1970s set off a wave of academic research that continues to this day. So, let's get started with our post-material philosophy for the future.[8]

Post-materialism is measured from data obtained through surveys that ask about respondent social priorities. Suppose you attach high priorities to such social goals as (1) protecting freedom of speech, (2) giving people more say in important government decisions, (3) seeing that people have more say about how things are done at their jobs and in their communities, (4) trying to make our cities and countryside more beautiful, (5) progress toward a less impersonal and more humane society, and (6) progress toward a society in which ideas count more than money. Then you are a post-materialist. Suppose instead you attach high priorities to such goals as (7) maintaining order in the nation, (8) fighting rising prices, (9) a high level of economic growth, (10) making sure this country has strong defense forces, (11) a stable economy, and (12) the fight against crime. In this case you are a materialist. If your priorities are mixed you lay on a spectrum in between. If your highest priorities are all materialist, that's what you are; if you highest priorities all go the other direction your are a post-materialist; if you have a mix of highest choice priorities you are neither.

Early research on post-materialism used just two post-materialist priorities, (1) and (2) above, and two materialist priorities, (7) and (8). Survey respondents were asked to choose between (1) and (7) and (2) and (8). The percent of the sample placed in the post-materialist category chose (1) and (2), while the percentage who chose (7) and (8) were placed in the materialist category, and the rest were counted as mixed. Later, a more complex set of questions using all twelve items became the research standard for developing a more refined index for measuring post-materialism.[9] Nonetheless, statistical research has confirmed that the simpler 4-question approach performs almost as well as do the 12-questions in measuring post-materialism.[10]

If you are in your twenties, you are more likely to be a post-materialist than if you are in your seventies. If you are young, you probably grew up in a period of economic prosperity, and if you are older you most likely faced economic deprivations in your pre-adult years. In general, younger generations today in Europe, America, and the prosperous Asian countries experienced secure economic conditions in their youth while older generations suffered material challenges when they were growing up. Because our basic values are formed by the time we reach adulthood, whether or not we face economic scarcity or social upheavals in our youth matters. As we age, our orientations fluctuate to some extent with economic conditions, but our basic outlook doesn't alter much. Those with materialist leanings in their youth keep them for life just as post-materialists retain their basic values. If we look at a cross-section of society today, younger birth cohorts tend to be more post-materialist than older, and, as time passes and younger replace older cohorts, the ratio of post-materialists to materialists increases in affluent, industrialized countries. In the early 1970s, materialists heavily outnumbered post-materialists in Western Europe, but by 2006 post-materialists slightly outnumbered materialists, and in the U.S. post-materialists by this time outnumber materialists by a ratio of 2 to 1. The most post-materialist country of all, Sweden, possesses a 5 to 1 ratio for post-materialists to materialists.[11]

Beginning recently in the 21st Century, younger birth cohorts in European countries became slightly less post-materialist than their immediate predecessor generations, probably because economic crisis and stagnation reduced economic prospects for new entrants job market entrants. Among the youngest adult generation in the U.S., post-materialism is under threat as well because of rising unemployment. Nonetheless, the post-material turn in affluent countries still looks to have plenty of life left in it despite recent economic setbacks. The U.S. economy is on the mend and economic optimism for the future is greatest among the youngest adults. Once Europeans get over their love affair with economic austerity and engage in expansionary government spending similar to the U.S., economic opportunities for younger generations will improve and they will likely recover from any angst about their material future and return to the post-materialist fold.

The brightest prospects for growth in post-material values lies in those countries that have yet to experience economic success. On the global stage, post-materialism bears a strong relationship to per capita incomes, as one would expect. Countries with high poverty rates and low income levels today have a strong materialist orientation, but as incomes increase across countries, the incidence of post-materialist values rises dramatically.[12] As countries develop and create conditions of economic security and political stability for their younger generations, the incidence of post-material values expands, even where affluence is new and novel. In China, for instance, post-materialist values have arisen amongst an emergent middle class and look to be more prevalent there than even in more affluent and democratic Taiwan.[13]

A shift to a post-material philosophy matters for everyday life. Post-materialism leads to a more outward social orientation and substantially enlarged demands for political expression, a consequence of inestimable importance around the world. Countries with a high incidence of post-materialism tend be strongly democratic, possess a high degree of tolerance toward homosexuality, promote gender equity, and rank high in interpersonal trust.[14] For post-materialists, freedom of self-expression is a big deal. Post-materialists also give substantial political support to both environmental protection and improvements in the quality of life through public action. The Green Party in Europe garners much of its support from citizens with post-materialist leanings.[15] Post-materialists are less supportive of older social issues involving unions and working class advancement, and don't always place themselves on a liberal-conservative political spectrum. The rise of the "independent voter" and post-materialism coincide, to which politicians increasingly need to pay attention in order to win elections. This means giving less truck to class issues and more to advancing social tolerance and the quality of life for all.[16]

We all possess a wider range of value orientations than those covered by post-materialist research, an essential conclusion of well-regarded survey studies by Israeli social psychologist, Shalom H. Schwartz, on what he calls "basics human values." These values include attitudes towards "power, achievement, hedonism, stimulation, self-direction, universalism, benevolence, tradition, conformity, and security." Universalism for Schwartz means "understanding, appreciation, tolerance, and protection for the welfare of all people and for nature," and benevolence refers to the "preservation and enhancement of welfare of people with whom one is in frequent contact." The other basic values have their expected, ordinary language meanings in Schwartz's work.[17] Although post-materialism encompasses a comparatively narrow range of social goals, it nonetheless correlates positively with the broader "basic human values" of universalism and self-direction, and negatively with a commitment to tradition and conformity, and a desire for personal security. In other words, many post-materialists express special concerns about both the welfare of all human beings and the natural world and put a high value on being self-directed, but don't like the straight jackets of too much security, social conformity, and tradition. Post-materialists also commonly lack strong attachment to self-enhancement values, such as power and achievement. In short, post-materialists possess a broad "other orientation" in their personal outlook as opposed to materialists who express their strongest commitments inwardly to achievement, security, and social conformity.[18]

Indices for "basic human values," such as "universalism," are constructed by Schwartz and other researchers by asking survey respondents to rank specific values as a guiding principle in one's life on a 1 to 9 importance scale. A universalism index, for instance, is created by averaging scores for the specific values of equality, social justice, environmental protection, unity with nature, inner harmony, world at peace, world of beauty, wisdom, and broad mindedness. Universalism, and other basic value indices, can in turn be correlated against a post-materialism index obtained from the same sample to test for statistical significance.[19]

Given their suspicion of orthodoxy and tradition, post-materialists don't warm easily to conventional religious practice, but this doesn't mean they lack spiritual inclinations. In Europe, where the trend to post-materialist values is especially strong, traditional religion is experiencing a sharp decline in popularity.[20] Taking its place appears to be an alternative spirituality which picks and chooses from a range of notions about the sacred. Instead of buying into pre-digested religious doctrines and subordinating the self to allegedly transcendent truths about the nature of being, spiritual practitioners increasingly rely on their own creativity to develop their patterns of belief. For a time, the so-called "New Age" movement, rooted in such phenomenon as astrology, reincarnation, fortune-telling, and contact with the dead, gained sway as a replacement for traditional religion, but New Age beliefs are on the wane. Instead, spiritual practices have become more amorphous and pragmatic with a heavy orientation to improving one's subjective experience of life where a connection to whatever is seen as a sacred is what really matters.

This new kind of spiritual phenomenon is variously referred to as post-Christian spirituality, or private or alternative religiosity, but it all is essentially the same phenomenon—a turn to spiritual beliefs and practices unaffiliated with any organized religion. Those who profess and practice an unaffiliated spirituality commonly hold post-materialist beliefs, including such untraditional views as support for gender equity, tolerance of a wide range of sexual behaviors, and the practice of non-hierarchical relationships within the family between parent and child. They often practice meditation and seek for a deeper and unconventional meaning of life free of existing doctrine, be it Christian or New Age. By contrast, religious traditionalists typically believe in a personal god, attend church, and belong to religious organizations, and new agers claim belief in astrology, reincarnation, fortune telling, or contact with the dead.[21] Spiritual individualists are more prone to post-materialist opinions about social priorities, express greater support for environmental protection, and have a higher level of educational achievement than either new agers or religious traditionalists.[22] One might think that post-materialists would be inclined to new age views, but New-Agers surprisingly have a conservative outlook on materialism akin to what one might expect of a low income, religious fundamentalism common in the U.S.

Let's take a moment to summarize post-materialism's content. Above all else, post-materialists value the right to self-expression in the lives of everyone and possess a high degree of social and cultural tolerance. Post-materialism itself is defined narrowly, but adherents oftentimes express other values that reflect an outward orientation to the world at large. The great modern challenge is finding common ground amongst a huge array of private interests and tribe-like attachments. Universalist values, which profess a concern for the welfare of humanity as a whole and for all of nature's beings, ease this challenge, and, fortuitously, post-materialists are often "universalists." Even though they lack an interest in conventional religion, post-materialists are not a bunch of atheists, but instead tend towards spirituality of an unorthodox kind. The big differences between liberal post-materialists and conservative materialists come in their respective attitudes towards society's institutions. While both post-materialists and conservatives subscribe to freedom of expression and the elimination of political oppression, conservatives express stronger attachments than liberals to hierarchies and authority, group loyalty, traditional religions and values, and limits on the role of the state in the economy and society. Liberal post-materialists to the contrary are skeptical of authority, hierarchy, and organized groups of any kind, avoid organized religion, and often take an untraditional path through life. While post-materialists sometimes express libertarian attitudes towards government, many take a pragmatic position about the necessity of government for providing essential public goods, restraining the excesses of a free market economy, and limiting religious oppression.[23]

Yet another way researchers look at shifting philosophical outlooks is to employ questions from the World Values Survey to measure orientations on a spectrum between survival, at the low end of a scale, and self-expression, at the high end, based on scaled response questions about (1) one's post-materialist-materialist orientation, (2) degree of happiness, (4) willingness to sign a political petition, (5) presence of a positive (as opposed to a negative) attitude toward homosexuality, and (6) level of trustfulness of others. A positive (high scaled) response to these items indicates a self-expressive orientation, while the opposite (low scaled) infers a survival orientation. Those who worry about survival are materialists, unhappy with their lives, unwilling to participate in politics, lack tolerance for homosexuality, and don't trust others, and self-expressers hold the opposite attitudes. The self-expression measure includes post-materialism, but goes beyond it. Studies using the World Values Survey confirm self-expresser support for gender equity, autonomy in the workplace, political freedom, and environmental protection, all of which comply with a "universalist" outlook for personal values. In survey research, the World Values Survey is a big deal because it covers so many countries with comparatively large population samples for each.[24]

Philosophical values documented in the World Values Survey turn out to not only fall on survival-self-expression continuum, but spread out along a traditional-secular/ rational spectrum as well. Traditionalists see (1) belief in God as important in their lives, (2) think children should be taught religious faith and obedience as opposed to independence and self-expression, (3) see pride in nationality as important, (4) have substantial respect for authority, and (5) oppose abortion. Rational secularists express the opposite values. Countries with strongly traditionalist values tend to score low on the survival-self-expression scale, but many of these, nonetheless exhibit a modest but steady trend to a self-expressive, post-materialist outlook over time. Specific religions score at different levels on the traditional-secular/rational scale, with Protestants tending to score high toward the secular end of the scale, Muslims low toward the traditional end, and Catholics in the middle.[25] Religion matters, but religious orientation does nothing to reverse the trend over time toward more prevalent self-expression values as more youthful post-materialist birth cohorts expand their population share. This is the case even for a highly traditionalist society such as Egypt.[26]

This doesn't mean that deeply Muslim countries will become bastions of liberal democracy and personal freedom anytime soon, but, simply, that there exists an underlying modest but inexorable movement of values in a more post-material, self-expressive, universalist direction. Nor does this mean that the red-blue state division in the U.S. will disappear quickly. The trend to post-materialism by its nature moves at a modest pace, especially in the U.S. and Europe where a strong contrary trend of population aging dampens political and cultural liberalization. The future will be post-material, but it won't arrive overnight.

While the formal study of actual human attitudes toward the meaning of life is a fairly recent human undertaking, philosophers have thought and written about what life means for centuries. Although academic philosophy has yet to venture into the world of empirical study, we should take advantage of the riches of historical philosophical thinking in interpreting the reality of public post-materialist attitudes. Let's give the language of the philosopher a chance in helping us sort out the meaning of life and a philosophy for the future in a practical way. We begin with the first philosopher who, above all, wanted to rewrite and reinvent the human values of his day, Friedrich Nietzsche. Stay tuned.

Chapter 4: Friedrich Nietzsche's Post-Material Philosophy

Friedrich Nietzsche, Friedrich Nietzsche, a cranky but brainy German philosopher who lived and wrote in the last half of the Nineteenth Century, wanted nothing to do with worries about final causes or pre-cooked religious explanations about ethics or the meaning of life. In his eyes freedom and autonomy are the central values to live by and meaning is to be sought in the experience of earthly existence. Religion is a con, a way for a priestly class to gain power over others, and ought to be chucked in favor of artistic expression as the medium for reconciling the sufferings and wonders of life. Simply put, in his thinking Nietzsche gives content to the bones of what today we call post-materialism, as we will now see.

***

The Greeks expressed two great themes in life: the beauty, power, and creativity of the human individual and the inevitability of deep and personal tragedy in the course of historical and personal events. The first took form in the plastic arts, in statues and temples, and the second in the Greek theater, in the performance of plays written in competitions to win the hearts of Greek audiences. The Greek spring theater festival commemorated Dionysus, the god of wine, a contradictory figure who at once purveyed the joys and ecstasies of life but also took pleasure in the chase of living beings and their dismemberment by his lovely maenads who otherwise danced and flitted through the woods in ecstatic revery. If nothing else, the Greeks are realists in the creation of their gods. Wine brings forth pleasure but also the dark ravings and destructiveness of dangerous drunks. Wine and celebration dulls life's rough edges but also can destroy its tranquility and beauty. Tragedy thus was a fitting theme for celebrating the emergence of new branches on the grapevine and the mixed blessing of the coming new wines.

The contrast of Apollonian orderly beauty and Dionysian ecstatic revery in Greek art and thought Friedrich Nietzsche describes brilliantly in his first book, *The Birth of Tragedy*.[27] On the topic of tragic pain and suffering, he knew of what he spoke. Illnesses, including migraines, deteriorating vision, and digestion problems, caused him to retire early from his professorship and kept him from studying and writing more than a few hours a day. He also sadly suffered from depression and mental disorders that eventually drove him insane.

Western thinking is wrongly dominated in Nietzsche's eyes by Socratic rational elements that exclude our darker non-rational side which takes form in a fear of death, a deep passion for life's pleasures, and the submergence of individuality within a larger being. The striving for continued existence, the exercise of the animal instincts, the lust for sexual union, and the mystery of death all possess an amazing power over our emotional lives. Just like the Greek god Dionysus, we want to immerse ourselves in these life forces, forget our individuality, and become one with the ecstasies of earthly being, but the danger is that such passions can get out of control and descend into the barbarisms of rape, pillage, and murder that we see all too often in the daily news.

The opposing and equally powerful tendency, to rationalize existence and explain it in logical terms, is embodied in Apollo, the Greek god of light, dreams, and plastic energy whose essence is captured by artists in sculpted, idealistic images that exhibit order, tranquility, and control. Apollo symbolizes regulated beauty and contentment, which Nietzsche sees as an illusion given the reality of tragic suffering and death, but an illusion that we all deeply desire. Otherwise, life's intrinsic pain would be too hard to bear. We dream of a predictable and beautiful world, and Apollo symbolizes that dream. Life for the Greek philosopher Socrates is Apollonian in its quest for truth through logical thought and orderly being. Wrong actions are the result of imperfect knowledge and good actions emerge from clear thinking; knowledge is virtue and the virtuous are happy.

In the original staging of Greek tragedy, the citizens of Athens shared a ceremonial and dramatic reconciliation with life's realities. Rather than narcissistically focusing on their individual plights, Athenians found collective dignity and joy in stories about life's deep sadnesses. We human beings long for connection with the primitive, the natural, and the wild, an ecstatic union with a worldly whole where we can forget our troubles. We would like to believe that we can control and shape the world and that doing so serves the end of our happiness. In reality we are limited beings with a modest capacity to determine our own destiny. Hard as it may be, we need to accept the cruelties of human existence and our individual limitations and find solace in earthly wonders. This is where joy and contentment come in—connection to the world and acceptance of our historical fate. Despite the horrors of daily life, we have little choice but to plunge ahead and do something that occupies our creative impulses. The collective experience of theatrical tragedy driven by the haunting music of the chorus helped the Greeks do just that. Music especially emotionally binds us to the group and lets us forget about our individual vulnerabilities. Psychologically it can put us in a trance and send us off to the heavens. For me personally, chamber music does the trick, but in our own times, the best example for most might be a rock concert, judging from audience behavior at such events. Any public gathering based on a shared experience give us an uplifting sense of connection to the human totality —baseball games, political rallies, plays (including Greek tragedies), and musical performances. We come away cleansed of daily irritations and feeling that life is good and worth living (unless maybe our team loses). Sporting events and political rallies satisfy our instincts to warrior competitiveness, and the performance arts our quest for beauty and order as well inoculation from life's pains and horrors. Public rituals and their underlying shared values create feelings of affinity and commitment within a society. After such events, one can return to daily life with a renewed energy to take on not only the ordinary but those Apollonian projects that give life an orderly grace and rationality. We indeed need a little 'Greek cheerfulness,' something that can give us comfort and joy in our personal lives to accompany our collective bond to the larger community and our reconciliation with our suffering and mortality. These are messages of *The Birth of Tragedy*.

***

Nietzsche's early thinking pivots on an interplay between individualistic creative impulses and the desire for a collective connection, but this is not to last. With the disappearance of Dionysian elements central to *The Birth of Tragedy* in his later writings, he turns to an individualistic, anti-metaphysical, and empirically oriented philosophy in such works as *Human, All-To-Human, The Dawn of Day,* and *The Gay Science*.[28] Understanding comes for him not from some other-worldly, overarching notion of a final cause, but through a close attention to the reality around us and a careful and critical assessment of humanity's social constructs and beliefs. Life in the world flows from interrelated chains of deterministic causalities, not from some singular underlying fundamental force. Quasi-religious, oceanic, or mystical feelings rooted in public spectacles or religious or artistic experiences are fine, but they tell us nothing about reality, other than the presence of a human inclination to such feelings. The need for collective connection to salve fears of suffering and death lacks earthly importance for the later Nietzsche in comparison to the significance of individual self-creation, to which the energies of our wilder Dionysian urges for sensual experiences and holistic merging are now to be sublimated, redirected, and put to good use.

This task constitutes a self-overcoming, a steering of one's emotional urges towards artistic and intellectual productivity. Out of this exercise in self-control arises the values that we should live by—courage, self-discipline, hardness, and intellectual integrity. One's personal life is like a work of art and should be consciously molded and shaped accordingly. We have to accept the fundamentals of who we are—our inner drives, our skills and talents, and our limitations—but we then must have the courage and will to consciously shape what we do in life. We shouldn't simply accept whatever society lays out for us as an income earner or consumer. If you don't like crunching numbers, avoid becoming an accountant. If you find the suburbs boring, take a chance and move to a more exciting but gritty central city. All this requires individual self-assertion and discipline, the opposite of succumbing to safe comforts and group conformity. Don't spend your life resenting and seeking revenge for what history has laid on you; focus instead on that one striving most stimulating to your passion and concern, and organize your being around it. This is the essence of Nietzsche's advice, not too different what one would find in the popular psychology section of a bookstore today. Self-creation in Nietzsche's eyes is only for those with a capacity to become "free spirits," a select group of elite thinkers willing to go against the social grain in their advocacy for new and unpopular ideas. "Free spirits" lead the charge in formulating unpopular but necessary alternatives to ossified and failed social traditions and institutions.

Nietzsche himself fills the bill as a "free spirit" in his unrelenting and lifelong attack on Christianity. The "death of God" claim, for which he is famous, refers uniquely to a Christian God and a doctrine that devalues actual existence in favor of a hypothetical and unproven afterlife. Faith in God and charity towards others in this life will be eternally rewarded in the next. One gives to a homeless beggar or the Salvation Army bell ringer at Christmas not out of fellow feeling, but from a fear of Godly retribution for being uncharitable, a sense of shame for being ungenerous, or the psychic satisfaction from feelings of economic superiority over recipients. The homeless beggar in turn experiences the indignity of having to rely on the charity of others. Nietzsche infers that charity of any kind, Christian or otherwise, blunts the desire for self-reliance, independence, and accomplishment, and insidiously debilitates cultural motivations for progress and achievement. Focusing on the next life supports the institutions of Christianity at the ultimate cost of weakening the cultural fabric of this life.

Although Nietzsche vigorously attacked modern Christianity, he recognized the need for tradition as a social glue essential for group survival in a world of conflict and competition. The medieval church, with the mystery of its ritual and the power of its priesthood to offer forgiveness of sins and entry into heaven, kept the peasantry under control and working hard to supply economic sustenance to religious elites and their aristocratic allies. Christian charity not only kept the church afloat, but also provided a safety net to the peasantry in hard times. For the majority of a society's population, what Nietzsche dismissively calls "the herd," obedience to the Christian tradition was essential for basic order in Medieval times, but in a changing world, such traditions lose their punch and new values are required to prevent cultural decline. In a modern capitalist society, economic discipline depends less on religious and more on economic reward. Belief in God and an afterlife loses its motivational functionality in today's consumer economy where more immediate benefits drive economic behavior.

In his explanation of how societies change and evolve, Nietzsche is a Darwinian. For survival, communities rely on a binding faith embodied in customs and traditions that create the order and civility essential for social survival. As a matter of habit individuals obey unwritten rules that limit harm to others in daily interaction and commit everyone to the defense of the community against outside oppression. We must not only be willing to hold doors for others and refrain from stealing wallets sticking out of back pockets, but to take up arms against our enemies if needed. From time to time, the basic tenants of the underlying binding faith lose their effectiveness, requiring the death of old traditions and the birth of new, and it is the "free spirits," those iconoclasts contemptuous of existing social arrangements, who successfully seek out new schemes essential for continued social progress. The values postulated in his day, especially by the church, were repulsive to Nietzsche, who saw in them as no more than a means for social domination. The "death of God" meant concretely to him the rejection of an existing religious dogma that, in its commitment to faith and charity, sapped the worldly passion for progress and creativity.

The notion of self-creating free spirits, who bring forth radically new schemes of social organization, doesn't jibe very well with Nietzsche's commitment to deterministic and naturalistic causal chains as key to understanding how the world works. If human life is a product of a Darwinian natural and historical determinism, then how can free spirits ever act to radically alter human values and change the course of history? One answer is the insertion of the "free spirit" as an adaptive force for change much like a genetic mutation. In a Darwinian social world, the probability of any "free spirit" causing dramatic historical shifts may well be infinitesimal but nonetheless positive just as the probability of any genetic mutation being evolutionarily adaptive is positive but very small. Cultural memes, ideas, symbols, and social practices that survive and get transmitted within a society from one person to another, bubble up in a random fashion much like adaptive genetic mutations. What a given free spirit accomplishes in creating such memes really doesn't matter much, but some one among many free-spirited ideas may stick and become the start of a larger social trend. With a sufficient number of functioning free spirits, chances are that someone will come up a new culturally adaptive value scheme essential to stave off social decline. A Darwinian world, whether biological or cultural, is still deterministic, but free spirits become a part of the adaptive dynamic through creation of cultural mutations. Whether Nietzsche was thinking in these terms I can't say. He may have inferred as much in the subtitle to his crowning literary achievement, *Thus Spoke Zarathustra: A Book for All and None*.[29] All of us should become the overman and creators of new notions, although no one of us is likely to be the one that changes the world, but we each have a shot at it. Modern reconciliations of free will and causal determinism places human rationality and intentionality within nature's causal determinism, and this Nietzsche accomplishes in his Darwinian take on evolutionary social change.

Aside from a commitment to free spirited self-creation and the death of heavenly explanations for being, Nietzsche is famous for a second theme, "the will to power," an idea that has received two interpretations, one benign and one insidious. At one level will to power is a self-overcoming, the guiding and directing of basic passions to productive ends. Self-creation of this kind requires a degree of will to power, but Nietzsche goes further and proclaims that there is within our earthly existence "will to power, and nothing besides." In this formulation, all of life becomes an exercise in self-expansion, power, and domination for individuals and societies alike. In his most foreboding work, *Beyond Good and Evil*, this idea takes on a special prominence.[30] In watching daily television newscasts on worldly events, one can easily become convinced that Nietzsche might be right.

For Nietzsche, a focus on will to power in some of his writings is more an experiment than an overarching commitment to a singular vision of human motivation. Throughout his intellectual career he tried ideas on for size and discarded those that didn't wear well. Some he simply put in the closet for later use, but as one Nietzsche scholar convincingly argues, "will to power" is not among them. The rise and fall of Nietzsche's commitment to will to power is chronicled in a chapter of a must-read book for anyone interested in philosophy, Julian Young's *Friedrich Nietzsche: A Philosophical Biography*.[31] Most tellingly, Nietzsche wrote over a thousand pages of notes on will to power but never published his planned crowning achievement on the topic. Nietzsche's sister Elizabeth deviously published a badly edited version, *The Will to Power: Attempt at Revaluation of All Values*, for her own ideological purposes after his death.[32] Otherwise, will to power as a singular notion explaining natural and historical evolution takes up very few of Nietzsche's published pages. That there is "will to power and nothing else" seems to be one of the ideas he tried on for size but ultimately rejected. Philosophers who achieve intellectual fame, such as Plato and Kant, are "systematizers" who create frameworks that claim to explain existence in comprehensive terms. Although he clamored for the recognition accorded systematizers, Nietzsche's deep intellectual integrity caused him to reject such an approach: "I mistrust all systematizers and go out of my way to avoid them."[33] The complexity and richness of the observed world precludes simplistic explanations and moves him to give up on will to power as an overarching idea of how things hang together. In *Twilight of the Idols*, one of his final published works, he expresses a renewed commitment to the behavioral dualism of the Dionysian urge for connection and the Apollonian impulse for individual creativity he originally described in *The Birth of Tragedy*.[34] Will to power remains in his thinking as a force behind personal self-overcoming and the impulse to free artistic and intellectual expression, but never fully takes hold as a final explanation of all organic and inorganic phenomena in the observed world. The path of human flourishing for Nietzsche is ultimately to be defined by a community's own invented virtues from which the brutal exercise of unbridled power will be excluded. Saying yes to life, no matter how tragic it may be, connects us to a world beyond the self. We follow our individual inclinations and desires, but among those is a need to further the continuation of life in whatever way we can, a force embodied in the overflowing power of the collective Dionysian urges. This is the final message of *Twilight of the Idols*, the single most compact statement of Nietzsche's philosophy.

The biggest flaw in Nietzsche's thinking for modern day liberals would be his attitude toward the masses of humanity, or as he called them, "the herd." The inference of the term is that the vast majority of human beings engage in a herd-like allegiance to cultural beliefs, in his day to a mindless Christianity, today perhaps to a mindless consumerism. He also refers to societies as a motley but uninteresting collection of cultural practices which lead nowhere. Nietzsche's essential goal was to be the one to lead western society to a promised land of recreated, coherent human values much as his fictional guru in *Thus Spoke Zarathustra*.[35] It is only the overman, the talented "free spirit," that is capable of pulling off leading the herd to becoming one with the Earth and giving up on heavenly rewards. For Nietzsche, it is Earth itself that contains all the wonders of being, and it is a human responsibility to preserve, enjoy, and advance earthly beauties and delights. This is the essence of Zarathustra's message. It is the Earth that is sacred, not the heavens. The real ambiguity in Nietzsche's thinking is the role of society's masses, or what he refers to as the "herd." Are they simply servants of free spirits? Cogs in an industrial wheel of material production? Nietzsche neither much liked the mechanisms of industrial capitalism nor trusted the state to bring about human liberation. He unrealistically suggests at one point that Europe's industrial masses seek their freedom through emigration to America, without really understanding that industrialism there differed little from Europe's. With his belief in democracy as a force for rule by the averageness of the herd, Nietzsche doesn't leave advocates of democratic pluralism much to go on. In the end, he calls not for democracy, but a society that serves a free-spirited philosophical elite, a vision not conceptually different from Plato's state ruled by a philosopher king. One could equally argue that a democratized world of free spirits, where everyone is self-creative and possesses the potential to produce adaptive social mutations, would lead more smoothly and consistently to positive social change than would a monopoly of elites. To come up with the notion of tolerance and equal rights for gays or protecting nature's wonders doesn't require a genius, just people who are clever and persistent, traits that I imagine are fairly widespread within humanity.

How do you know when life has achieved its self-creative purpose? Nietzsche offers us a mental exercise to establish just this. Suppose you are told that you will experience your life in its every detail repeatedly in a never ending cycle. Would you view this news with absolute horror or overpowering joy? This is an expression of Nietzsche's doctrine of the "eternal return of the same." If this question evokes positive feeling, then you must be close to your self-creative goal. Most of us do things we seriously regret, but if we can look back on our life as a whole and judge it positively, we have done the best we can. Nietzsche's eternal return is a tough taskmaster most of us can never perfectly satisfy. Nonetheless, Zarathustra in Nietzsche's crowning literary work experiences spiritual and Dionysian visions of eternal return through an ecstatic connection to his free-spirited disciples, as imperfect in practice as they were. Nietzsche here closes his own intellectual circle with a return to the idea of submergence in the whole. In an act of self-overcoming we are to organize our life around a singular mission that links us to the historical fate of the world around us. Our chosen mission, would allow us to will eternal return, not just for ourselves but for all that exists. My reading of this point goes something like this: choose a mission for your life that you believe would be good beyond your own self; organize you life around that mission; while having an ultimate faith that your hopes will be realized, bear no illusions that your personal accomplishments will make much difference, but retain a lifelong commitment to the end you seek. No matter how painful and fearful life is, to it one must always say yes. In Nietzsche's eyes, this is the essential message of the Greeks who individually and collectively celebrated human perseverance, heroism, and perfection in the face of overwhelming cruelty and tragedy.

Nietzsche's aphoristic style of writing, although engaging, challenges the reader to come up with a coherent vision of what he is up to. About this, there is much debate, but I personally find Martin Heidegger's conclusion on Nietzsche in *What is Called Thinking?* to be especially useful.[36] According to Heidegger, the central message of *Thus Spoke Zarathustra* is that man is unready to assume responsibility for the power of industry and technology and as a result is turning the Earth into a "wasteland." Man is not yet capable of thinking clearly about his existential reality and is still prone to look beyond the Earth to the heavens for his salvation. Nietzsche's clear-thinking "overman" will instead look to the realities of life on Earth in the creation of meaning, not to the unreality of an afterlife in the great beyond. True "free spirits" will seek not just their personal pleasures, but will set the Earth itself up as a truly sacred being to be respected and loved. Its not too much of a stretch to claim that Zarathustra was an environmental philosopher who, by proclaiming the death of God, wants to pull our attention back to the wonders of the world in which we actually live. The "overman" will be both a humanist and environmentalist and therefore a post-material universalist.

***

If Nietzsche lived today, where would he find his "free spirits"? Given his passion for the arts, especially for music, he would doubtlessly check out the post-materialists bringing new energy and artistic accomplishment to some of our older central cities. Here he might find fascination with the emergent quest for creative accomplishment in both the arts and digital arenas, growing distaste for conformity to the materialist values, Dionysian desire for unique collective and personal experiences, and growing advocacy for free personal expression. He might be pleasantly surprised by post-materialism's combination of stylistic nonconformity and traditional commitment to hard work and merit-based reward at places like Google and Facebook. While Nietzsche would not find the democratic informality of the digital world very appealing, he might like its creativity and unconventionality. While Google seems to at least give lip service to respecting and protecting the earth's wonders, whether the Google folks satisfy Nietzsche's vision of the overman as a protector of the Earth we cannot say.

While he always fascinates in his writings, Nietzsche doesn't always leave much for the soul. As close as he comes is his talk of "spiritualizing" our basic human drives for sex and love, warfare, or ecstatic communal celebrations instead of sublimating and suppressing such urges in deference to some distant, heavenly god and unnatural morality. Much like the Greeks, who created their gods in their own image, sexual promiscuities and all, Nietzsche calls for a humanized spirituality. He speaks of the Earth itself in a sacred tones and wants it treated as such, and he emphatically says yes to earthly life as tragic and painful as it can be. To traditional religionists, such talk would be a sacrilege, but not so much to post-materialists who express a spirituality unattached to any particular doctrine. Martin Heidegger, another controversial but brilliant German philosopher, who also mistrusts metaphysicians and systematizers, takes Nietzsche's notion of a philosophy and spirituality rooted in the realities of daily life even further, as we will now see. Stay tuned.

Chapter 5: Martin Heidegger's Being in the World and the Stewardship of Nature

Being a post-materialist means that in deciding how to live one goes beyond a narrow focus on private economic interests to include such purposes as individual self-expression, social tolerance, and a quality environment. While suspicious of organize religion, many post-materialists adhere to an unstructured form of spirituality and express a sense of the sacred. For this reason, it is time to extend our philosophy for the future to account for such an emotional attachment to something larger than the self. The one philosopher that accomplishes this while avoiding the metaphysics of final causality or reliance on belief in a creator, is Martin Heidegger. We will see in Heidegger's writings a philosophy that treats the everyday universe of perception with a non-religious spiritual reverence and a deep conviction that calls out for the preservation of both humanity's and nature's earthly wonders.

***

Most of us rarely think about what 'being in the world' truly means and leave such questions to academics or theologians. We need to get on with our daily lives where most of the issues we face are pragmatic. For philosophically oriented speculative thinkers, to ask about the nature of being is the most elevated of all questions, but also the most difficult to grasp. To emphasize the importance of the question, let's follow Heidegger and capitalize 'Being' just as it is our common practice to capitalize 'God' when we speak of beliefs in a final creator. Particular beings include all the phenomenon of human experience—Cormorants diving for fish in Lake Michigan, light reflecting on water from a morning sun peaking through the clouds, bikers head to work on a bike trail, the taste of espresso, and whatever else enters your consciousness. We can postulate one common element of all such beings without getting into too much philosophical trouble—all things in our field of perception exist at the moment we observe them. Being in this sense refers to the active presence of an endless array of particular objects and their interconnections, but not to any abstract, and probably unanswerable, questions about ultimate cause. In making this claim, we direct our attention to the perceived as such and to the simple amazement of its existence. This I think is what Heidegger is up to, but I will leave the final judgment about this to you once we summarize some of his philosophical ideas.

For Martin Heidegger, to ask about the nature of Being is to look closely at life as we find it. He grew up in intensely Catholic and conservative early Twentieth Century rural southern Germany where his father was a master cooper and sexton of the local Catholic Church. Heidegger's education through the university level was paid for by the Church with the expectation that he was destined for the clergy. At the university in Freiburg, he shifted from preparation for the priesthood to the study of Catholic philosophy, receiving a scholarship from the church in support of his work. Heidegger rejected Catholicism soon after World War I and moved on to become a student of the phenomenologist Edmund Husserl, gaining a position as a professor at (the Protestant) Marburg University and ultimately succeeding Husserl at Freiburg in 1928. By this time Heidegger's lectures in philosophy were the stuff of legend in German intellectual circles.

Heidegger published his much anticipated book, *Being and Time*, in 1927.[37] Here he sets out the work that is to occupy him for the rest of his life, the sorting out of the meaning of being in the world. To a pragmatic thinker, this would seem to be a self-indulgent exercise in abstract theorizing, but what Heidegger attempts to create is a philosophy of everyday life, a task that begins with sorting out the significance of the different objects we encounter.

Those that rise to particular importance are the "ready-to-hand": the tools of existence—hammers, plows, houses, computers, cups and saucers, coats and pants, guitars, baseballs, and so on. The rest of the things we encounter, the "present-at-hand," lay in the background of our lives and fail to attract our attention because we don't care much about them—beetles, sphagnum moss on forest trees, boulders, discarded plastic bags. Something of little interest to us at one point in our life may take on a special significance at another; a rock of a certain size becomes especially important to me when I want to pound tent stakes into the ground on backpacking trips. We approach any object in our attention span with "circumspection." How can we use it? Will it harm us in some way? Is it pleasing? How does it function? What does it do? How do I avoid it or get around it?

Given the social nature of human experience, our encounters with human-others, as opposed to objects, takes on a special importance, and is referred to as "being-with." One's everyday life consists of a complex of interrelationships with others—spouses, children, grocers, car mechanics, beauticians, baristas, friends, lovers, fellow workers, softball teammates. We approach these individuals with "solicitude." How do others react to my behavior? Do I trust someone? Am I sexually attracted to a particular person? Is my softball teammate a skilled player? Does this barista make really good espresso? How can I help my son become less depressed? Is the police officer following me going to give me a ticket? Will I be assaulted if a go into a particular neighborhood? Will my friends be at the coffee shop today?

The vast majority of our relations in the world, both with humans and nonhuman objects, take on an ordinary quality, or "everydayness." I get up, have breakfast with my wife, maybe talk about plans for the day, read some of the newspaper, go exercise, head to the coffee shop, haul out my computer to do some writing (I am retired), go home for lunch, chat and gossip with people I know at another coffee shop, read some philosophy, shop at the grocery store, fix dinner, talk about my day with my wife, and so on. These are the repetitive, ordinary tasks of daily existence. In them, one life looks much like another; nothing distinguishes us or causes us to stand out. We gain enjoyment from many of these activities and connections, although not all. I love conversing with friends on the horrible state of politics or the economy, or talking to the barista about the finer points of making espresso, but I am not so keen about calming my son's anxieties around having to learn college level economic theory, or having to speak with a neighbor about a dent I put in his car when backing out of my driveway. I enjoy fixing dinner and having a glass of wine while doing so, and I like catching the evening news. Some of what we do may be quite boring, although necessary to daily life—washing the dishes, getting the laundry done, painting the deck, commuting on a congested expressway, serving the fiftieth cup of coffee to our customers at work, and numerous other tasks you can imagine for yourself. Of course boredom and its lack is partly a matter of taste—I thoroughly enjoy hanging laundry outdoors on a summer's day, something many think to be intrinsically mundane.

Your hackles may rise at the idea that the ordinary experiences that take up much of our earthly existence are "inauthentic," but that's what Heidegger calls them. He does this not to denigrate the ordinary. After all, most of the events of our life are pretty ordinary, but that doesn't mean they are unnecessary or that the don't bring us joy. I love my daily espresso, but that doesn't mean it is anything special in the bigger scheme of things. Ordinary life can be good, but it isn't what gives us our unique identity. What does this is the "authentic," that generally rare kind of activity that causes us to stand out from the crowd and puts into practice our own, self-determined philosophy of life. To live fully, is to both live in everyday inauthenticity and to express one's idiosyncratic and "authentic" self.

The essential human motivation underlying both the everyday and the authentic is "care." As already noted, we approach life with circumspection, concern, and solicitousness. We care about those things and those persons in the environment around us that we take to be important. We fear having the things we need and the people close to us torn away. There is nothing necessarily altruistic in the idea of care. Care can be about the self; one can care deeply about avoiding muggers lying in wait in dark alleys, or a homeless person can feel serious concern about where her next meal will come from; or care can be for the well-being of others close to us, or for the place or community in which we live, or for things in the natural world we have come to love like wildflowers and beautiful landscapes. Care is an existential feature of life. I care; therefore I am.

Closely related to care is the idea of "anxiety." Anxiousness is a kind of nebulous fear about not-being, about being a nothing rather than a something. One goes through daily life without thinking much about nonexistence, but in reflective moments one suddenly becomes fearful of not living, or, more to the point, not having lived in a significant way. We become worried about sinking into the obscurity of the average in our daily being. This is the source of our inherent, if often hidden, desire to go beyond everydayness and seek something authentic. Anxiety generates a particular form of care—a special concern about having a personal existence that is uniquely valuable. Recognizing the possibility of "not being" creates anxiety about finitude in our lives, but its flip side, the mere fact that beings exist, can also create "astonishment" and wonder. Such astonishment is as fundamental as anxiety. We awake each day with a feeling of anxiousness about what it is we should do, or with a feeling of amazement that we exist in a world where the sun shines through our window, or maybe both. Out of our conflicting emotions, we carve out a balance between care for everydayness and a passion for something special, that is if we are both resolute and lucky.

Authenticity in its essence is subjective. We can debate about what an authentic life is like, but we cannot establish final standards to describe it. One can speak of authenticity in a general way, but not be able to say for sure if this or that person attains it. Whether one's own actions are authentic is a matter of reflective, honest self-judgment. We can, and do in our public discourse, look at the lives of others and argue about the character of their actions. Read newspapers, websites, and advertisements —most say something about questions of personal authenticity. People whose lives have authentic elements get written about, but not so much those stuck in inauthenticity. Who would admit to living a mundane life of total everydayness? People do own up to unhappiness in the extensive survey research on the subject, but do unhappiness and inauthenticity go together? One can be dumb and happy, as the saying goes, one could be inauthentic and happy as well, or even authentic and miserable. The best way to describe the authentic is that unique part of our own life that we pursue as a matter of passion and special commitment. The authentic rises above the mundane and becomes a special kind of activity, an act of free expression. This doesn't mean that we escape everydayness in our existence; it simply means that at some moments we engage in something more. We are all moved to live authentically, but some no doubt do this more successfully than others. This is why we take such an interest in the topic. We all in some way want to stand out and express our own individuality, but we also enjoy submerging ourselves into the comforting routine of our everyday being.

Both everydayness and authenticity exist in the context of concrete daily existence and thus possess "historicality." To speak about history from the individual's perspective is to talk about a unified self that exists over time. At the core of our identity is a selfsameness we create by knitting together sequences of experiences into a kind of personal narrative. We desperately want to have a story we can tell others that expresses the meaning of our particular existence. This is how we become historical.

For the most part, we exist within the facts of history. Our possibilities are given to us by what our culture and time delivers up. We are tossed into a world not of our making, but in this world we can behave resolutely and rise above everydayness by committing ourselves to a heritage, a certain set of time-tested practices. We are compelled by fate to take the plate we are given, but we can choose what we take from it. In short, we can't alter history writ large, but we can shape our own personal destiny within it.

In accepting a tradition we buy into a certain vision of how a particular kind of life should be lived. Some traditions deserve to die, even to be destroyed. Choosing from history's plate can be exceedingly dangerous without an intense and open public debate about what should be rejected out of hand. Any tradition with the clear potential to demean, enslave, and destroy human and other natural beings on its face is a candidate for such rejection. Heidegger himself flirted with Nazism, a mistake most scholars say he has tragically failed to fully acknowledge. We as human individuals choose from what we are given, commit ourselves to certain traditions and values, shape and alter them to the degree that we can, and pass them on. One can unquestioningly and inauthentically accept the prevailing popular conceptions of culture, or one can actively and authentically seek to carve out one's own unique interpretation of how life ought to be lived. This doesn't mean totally rejecting the offering of history but taking it as a starting point for creative and idiosyncratic departures. The ultimate requirement for doing this is reasonable practical freedom and the ultimate responsibility is to avoid harm to others and work to expand the freedom of all for authentic pursuits. Heidegger hues more closely to the offerings of history in his discussions of how to live than free-spirited Friedrich Nietzsche who is quick to reject ossified historical traditions and argue for the creation of radically new social practices that serve human creativity.

Let's take a moment to summarize Heidegger's essential position so far. We approach questions of being in the world with an amorphous anxiety and trepidation about our own existential status. Our tendency is to ignore such questions precisely because of the stress they create and trundle on with our lives. On this path, we will never feel quite at home in the world in Heidegger's eyes. To live more authentically and honestly, we need to face up to life's painful realities and in a sense transcend our everydayness by imagining the possibility of nonexistence. This is our ultimate horror, not being, and the source of our most obscure but most troubling sense of anxiousness. It's as if we could take a trip out to the edge of some ultimate black hole with the power to suck us up into nothingness and look into its throat. But also from such an imagined perspective we can look back at the universe of our existence. What else could we feel but wonder, amazement, astonishment?

**

Productive and creative acts in Heidegger's eyes originate not just in human endeavors, but start from nature itself. In high mountain meadows when the snow melts in spring, plants emerge from the soil, leaf out to draw energy from the sun, and push forth beautiful flowers to attract bees or hummingbirds that will move pollen from one plant to another thereby activating the reproductive process that will assure a next generation of plants.[38] Human creative activity simply helps along what is already latent in the world of nature. A piece of fine-grained wooden furniture emerges through the work of an artisan from the wood of a large, old tree cut from the forests. Crops spring forth from soils sown by human hand but driven by the energy of the sun. The work of a sculptor unfolds a statue from a large piece of marble created by the forces of nature. The power of the wind turns a windmill placed in its path to generate electricity for human use. What human beings do in their everyday working life helps nature along in the creation of objects of utility and value. Humanity and nature act together as partners in an ecological world to create those material objects that satisfy human wants and desires.[39]

Such a naturalized, and some might say romanticized, view of human productive activity on its face has little to do with the reality of the modern industrial society where, with little thought given to nature's creativity, materials ready-to-hand get forcibly extracted from the earth and chemically and mechanically recombined into objects of utility. In the modern industrial world everything becomes strictly a resource, a standing-stock, and this includes human activity. Human beings direct the process of cranking out powerful motor vehicles, cell phones, laptops, digital sounds and images, and ready-to-eat fast food, but they also functions as cogs in the gears of production. We may feel in control of the assembly system for Ford Explorers or applications for Apple ipads, but in practice the underlying technology is a legacy of a long string of scientific discoveries, engineering achievements, and business practices. At any point in history we are given the technological system available and can tweak it at the margins, but cannot invent it totally anew. In short, we each become but a small piece in a historically given technical and economic system that we are powerless to alter. Now there is nothing wrong with being both an object within, and a subject who directs, productive activity—after all this is what humans have done in most of their waking hours throughout history. The real issue is whether technology and the economy take over our entire living being, or whether we recognize and enjoy a life and a world beyond the purely material. To cave into the strictly economic in Martin Heidegger's view is to confine oneself to inauthenticity. Instead we should look beyond the economic horizon to a larger world of natural marvels with an existence of its own to which we owe an obligation of concern and care. The trap of the modern age is a total human absorption in the amazements that modern technology produces and the ignoring of the even greater amazements that lie beyond the human economic skin. How does one avoid such an entrapment?

The antidote to an inauthentic economic reality is to somehow change our daily work routine to allow us to experience and celebrate the world as a fragile, precious, and wondrous place. Technology needn't be an independent, overpowering force so long as we organize it in such a way as to respect nature's own unfolding and wonders, to see our own actions as the completion of a larger natural process, and to allow our creative impulses to be realized in the production of items and activities not just of utilitarian value, but that connect us to the marvels of Being itself. We all indeed are resources, but we are more than that. We have the privilege of being able to contemplate the world around us and find in it meaning and beauty. The answer to economic and technological dominance is not Luddism, but to instead transform the economy and technology and render it secondary to the sacredness of existence and beings. One can make use of science and technology without intervening in natural processes for the sole purpose of controlling and exploiting them. Similarly, one can function in the economic arena without disregarding the creative impulses, both natural and human in origin.

Despite such possibilities, technological and economic predominance in our lives is more a matter of fate rather than personal desire according to Heidegger. None of us have explicitly chosen the economic world we live in. It has simply emerged as a product of the small actions of millions of people over a long span of time. Modernity, where everything is a pure resource and our energies go into endless rounds of producing and consuming, holds sway as a matter of current historical destiny, but this needn't rule out a different future. Treating everything as a pure resource and being stuck on an economic treadmill isn't inevitable.

While we individually lack the capacity for implementing a new economic vision society-wide, we do have a degree of personal choice in the way we live. We can in our daily life move beyond entrapment in consumerism and technology and reintroduce the mystery of Being into our actions. We can individually be "free spirits" who live unconventionally, demonstrating to others the possibility of a personal turning to a new way of being. Eventually, the political weight of those who follow a different vision could be enough to politically create a larger move to new arrangements that overcome technological determinism and allow for a more authentic mode of earthly existence. Living one's values in such circumstances inadvertently shapes a larger destiny and could be akin to a communicable virus that can move at lightening speed. The Tunisian and Egyptian revolutions brought forth by "youthful free spirits" attuned to modern communication technology suggests the possibility of a quick and radical turn to a democratic future and away from autocratic rule. How this new movement will pan out remains to be seen, especially in light of Egypt's recent counter-revolutionary coup, but for the moment fatalism has died in the Middle East.

***

To move beyond a life where the economy holds sway requires something to move towards, which we can discover by expanding our perceptual horizons to take in the idea of dwelling—living in the world in a truly human manner—an idea that Heidegger develops in his later writings.[40] To dwell is to feel safe and cared for in the place where one resides, and to actively care for those others and things that make up this place. To care for something is to passively and actively let it be, to let it unfold itself in accordance with its own nature. In short, we should tune into the wonders of all those beings around us in our dwelling place and extend our care to them as manifestations of the marvels and mystery of existence.

The everyday meaning of the term 'dwelling' is to live in a locality, a place in close proximity to work, schools, shopping and entertainment, friends, and nature's wonders. Dwelling takes on a deeper significance when we do more than just reside in a locality but feel special emotional ties to its environment and way of life. In the presence of such ties, our expressions of care will take form as letting local dwellers seek their self-creative paths through life, a town or city develop according to community needs, architecture fit the aesthetic and natural features of the local landscape, a river follow its own created path, and native flora and fauna play out their evolved natural relationships. To dwell in a deeper sense doesn't mean we forego treating beings as resources—we need resources to live—but to recognize that they possess value and interest in their own right regardless of their resource status.

Dwelling takes more specific form by thinking in terms of the "fourfold": earth, sky, mortals, and divinities (in Heidegger's words). "Earth" and "sky" refer to our natural environment including all its living and nonliving beings and their interconnections. "Mortals" refers not only to our membership as citizens of a larger ecological community, but also to our special presence as self-conscious, thinking, mortal, social beings who have the special capacity to question the meaning of all that we encounter. The final piece of the fourfold, and perhaps the hardest to understand, is the "divinities." One's immediate reaction would be to interpret these as the gods of organized religions, but this is not solely what Heidegger has in mind. Rather, the divine constitutes an unwritten community ethos manifested in the lives of its cultural heroes. Heroes lack divinity in the ordinary religious sense, but they embody in their histories and outlooks values that we hold dear—freedom, justice, courage, care, and generosity. Against our heroes, we judge the content of our own lives. The idea of divinities as framing our lives contains a second more intangible element—an attitude of sacredness towards all of beings.

In any lament of the modern condition and its absence of authentic dwelling, technology takes center stage. Technology itself today is encased in a larger economic system fired by constant innovation. The driving force is not just technology, but an extensive media apparatus that entices human consumers to the latest gadgets or symbols of beauty, power, or status that technological forces create. In this arrangement, the powers of technology get directed to stimulating and fulfilling the siren song of consumer craving and satisfaction.

To find authentic meaning and to dwell fully in the world, in Heidegger's thinking we need to look beyond the horizons created by technology and the economy. To illustrate his meaning, he contrasts the constructing of a bridge and a dam. Building a well-designed bridge to connect two riverbanks and their associated landscapes and human communities is an act of dwelling that preserves a river's natural flow and provides a setting that can inspire thoughts of larger connections to humanity and nature, Earth and sky. Building a dam that converts a flowing river into a lake runs counter to authentic dwelling by unnecessarily destroying a natural being. Today electric energy can be generated instead by the blowing wind or the shining sun. One needn't irrevocably harm the processes of nature in the use of it as a resource, nor be a Luddite to save nature's wonders.

To live authentically one must make a concrete choice about how to live. Since alternative options from which to choose are already largely established by the forces of history, starting with a clean slate in constructing a life is impossible. Heidegger himself was born into a heritage of conservative rural Catholicism and began his career as a Catholic philosopher, but he soon left the church and sought to broaden his thinking beyond the constraints of religious doctrine. He adopted the language of the philosophical thought of his day, but took it in a sharply new direction. Accepting a particular way of thinking doesn't necessarily mean a rigid adherence to past doctrines. A tradition can serve as a starting point for moving in a new direction as Heidegger demonstrates in his own life as an intellectual.

We all are pushed and shoved about by the contingencies of history, but we can resolutely face up to life's realities and choose that part of our historical inheritance that gives our own life meaning. Much of what we do falls in the realm of the ordinary (Heidegger would say inauthentic as we already noted), but we can still openly choose those values and practices that we judge, on serious reflection, to be especially worthy. Whether this includes elements of a religious tradition is up to us. To select a phenomenon that bears repeating is to adopt a heritage we would want to pass on to the future—the age old rituals of the Catholic Church or the Muslim faith, or perhaps a spiritually oriented environmentalism that sees nature as an amazing and sacred living organism. The choice of an existing tradition does not preclude innovation and creativity in our lives. We can participate in Catholic or Muslim rituals while at the same time advocating for a halt to greenhouse gas emissions, family planning to stabilize global population, or gender equity. To accept a tradition doesn't necessarily mean we have to buy its outmoded details. Nor need we accept prevailing social practices. As post-materialists have discovered, construction of one's own unique spirituality and notion of the sacred remains an open possibility.

Resoluteness is key in making such choices. We can simply go with the flow of popular culture and choose beliefs and practices put forth by others, or we can look carefully at our lives and decide for ourselves what's truly important. A women freely choosing to wear a burqa daily with all but her eyes covered as a sign of faith would be acting resolutely to shape her destiny, but would behaving irresolutely if she simply allowed such a practice to be thrust upon her. Nietzsche, the "free spirit," takes an unequivocal position on the question of such choices—when in doubt, get rid of oppressive traditions. Freely choose those that make for a creative life. Heidegger is not so explicit on the standard for choosing what to retain and what to reject.

A heritage for Heidegger is bound up in his notion of divinities. Earth and sky serve as metaphors for the mysteries of nature and the larger universe. World encompasses all the relationships, both cultural and natural, we face as mortal beings. Divinities embody the stories we tell ourselves about the origin and meaning of life and how we should live it. They are the heroes whose lives we choose to emulate. For Heidegger, we psychologically look back to all that we perceive in world from the vantage point of looking into the abyss of not-being with both deep anxiety and amazement. From this perspective, we adopt and create traditions and values about how to live. Heidegger infers in us a deep desire to care for beings, but he infers nothing about the existence of God. He is providing a perspective about Being, not a final truth about its content except to say that we all should in some dimension of our life be true stewards of the Earth and its occupants.

For any of us moderns who look outside of our personal boundaries towards the world itself for life's meaning, Heidegger is telling us about our need to spiritualize that which gives us a sense of amazement about our existence. To post-materialists having a universalist attachment to both humanity and nature, Heidegger's philosophy directly speaks.

Chapter 6: Post-material Meaning and Downtown Living

If post-materialist meaning motivates a growing middle class interest in high-density, compact urban living, and evidence suggests that it does, then post-materialists must find special satisfactions in a compact urban environment they don't get elsewhere. How exactly can spatial compactness facilitate post-materialist pursuits? Let's get down to Earth in exploring the practical consequences of a post-materialist future. A newly adopted philosophy of how we live has concrete consequences for how history will unfold. Let's see how this could be the case and how philosophy truly matters and isn't just for intellectuals to puzzle over.

Jean-Paul Sartre, French author, playwright, and philosopher, loved Paris and spent most of his life there. He lived in modest accommodations as a young man, earned his living teaching, and spent much of his day in cafes, writing, meeting with students, and talking with fellow intellectuals. During World War II, he could be found daily at the seedy Cafe de Flore next to the stove (only cafes could get coal for heat) near the Sorbonne where he had received his degree in philosophy. He first gained public attention with the publication of his existentialist novel *Nausea* in the 1930s and soon saw his plays, such as "No Exit," being performed in Paris theaters. Right after the war, Sartre was invited to defend his existentialist philosophy at the Club Maintenant near the Grand Palais where he had to push his way through an overflow crowd to get to the podium. Sartre uses Paris and its cafe life as a backdrop not only for his novels and plays, but even to illustrate philosophical points in his famous *Being and Nothingness*.

Anyone, such as Jean-Paul Sartre, whose passion in life requires a cheap place to live, inexpensive and efficient public transit, cafes where one can linger all day for the price of a cup of coffee, personal interaction with likeminded others, access to a highly specialized audiences or markets for the fruits of one's labor, or public institutions such as museums, theaters, stadiums, gymnasiums, universities, or libraries will be attracted to high density urban living. It is in densely packed older cities where such needs are best satisfied. Add to this a decent nightlife, good restaurants, bustling and architecturally interesting neighborhoods, and attractive parks where one can enjoy a bit of nature, and you have most of the ingredients of an "urban" as opposed to a "suburban" dream.

In my own city, two older, densely populated neighborhoods, Riverwest just to the north of downtown and Bayview just to the south, contain a mix of century-old, moderate single family houses, duplexes, and apartments, and numerous aging commercial and industrial buildings. These two neighborhoods have become a haven for students, artists, activists, teachers, and a variety of others whose aspirations or incomes preclude living in the suburbs. Riverwest is the birthplace of Lakefront Brewery, a successful producer of microbrews, and Bayview is home to innovative storefront cultural venues such as the Alchemist and Boulevard Theaters. In both neighborhoods, one can find great new restaurants, cafes, bars, art galleries, organic food cooperatives, and funky stores. Alterra, a rapidly growing local coffee roaster, recently constructed an architecturally innovative roasting facility and cafe in Riverwest, and just opened a huge, visually stunning new cafe in Bayview with a big bakery in view of customers who to get watch the action. Bayview is blessed with close access to a beautiful Lake Michigan shoreline park, and Riverwest borders great hiking trails along a revitalized natural Milwaukee River corridor. Riverwest is also less than a mile from the University of Wisconsin-Milwaukee (UWM) campus. Owning and using an automobile in these neighborhoods is a pain given the limits on parking, and one can get around easily walking or biking. Milwaukee lacks fancy light rail for public transit, but we do have a fairly functional bus system. Residents of Riverwest or Bayview don't really need to bear the expense of car ownership, and they can reside in fairly decent housing more cheaply than in Milwaukee's suburbs. Crime remains a problem, but it is on the decline in both neighborhoods. If you aspire to the materialist amenities of the suburban dream, Riverwest and Bayview aren't for you. But if you are looking beyond financial accomplishment and material possessions for meaning in life, either of these neighborhoods might be the place you would want to live.[41]

It isn't just the offbeat older neighborhoods of Milwaukee that are on the rebound, but more upscale developments in and around downtown as well, such as the city's Third Ward, an old wholesale district with architecturally unique buildings dating from the late Nineteenth Century. Here rising urban popularity has stimulated conversions of older buildings to offices and middle class dwellings with street level retailing alongside new condominium construction. Young affluent professionals and suburban expats drive this trend and they seem more interested in luxury consumption than the residents of Bayview or Riverwest judging from the pricy boutiques and expensive restaurants springing up in the Third Ward and elsewhere downtown. The Third Ward hosts a public market and a performing arts complex home to the Skylight Opera and two theater companies that specialize in modern and experimental plays. Today, the revitalized Third Ward attracts both upscale local residents and tourists to its galleries, restaurants, bars, and entertainment venues, although at the sacrifice of some of its original seedy charm.

The essential virtue of compact urban living is close spatial proximity to diverse, interesting urban neighborhoods and a variety of public and private enterprises including theaters, markets, libraries, parks, and institutions of higher learning. The fundamental advantage of expansive suburban living is the comforts of space manifested in big houses and yards, wide roads, and large, auto-accessible shopping malls. The suburbs facilitate material aspirations; diverse densely packed cities foster a broad spectrum of pursuits, some material in orientation, and some not. Great cities of the world contain their temples of consumption filled with material treasures for the wealthy, but they also contain wonderful street markets and numerous small enterprises where the desires of the palate and other simple pleasures find satisfaction at a reasonable price. One needn't be affluent to enjoy the virtues of high-density urban living and to follow a post-materialist path through life, but if you are a prosperous professional or retiree more interested in stimulating experiences than consumer acquisitions, and require or desire close proximity to like-minded others, then the downtown living may well be for you.

***

Richard Florida, a regional science professor, has gained star standing among urban planners for his book, *The Rise of the Creative Class*.[42] Florida presents evidence for the emergence of an economically important group of individuals with a new take on life that bears the marks of post-materialist thinking and plays a driving role in a renaissance of downtown urban revitalization. According to Florida, the creative class is compose of professionals, such as scientists, engineers, university professors, poets, novelists, entertainers, designers, architects, and opinion-makers, who conceive new intellectual or artistic forms of economic or public value. Members of the creative class are at once bohemian and conformist, like the Google and Facebook people we talked about earlier. They have an intense desire for personal self-expression, which includes body-piercing jewelry and tattoos, but also possess a powerful work ethic and passion for personal accomplishment, especially in the digital arena doing software development or graphic arts. These are the people one increasingly sees sitting around gourmet coffee shops huddled over their computers or conversing in small groups about a website design, solving a computer software problem, pulling off the conversion of an old commercial building into condominiums, or getting someone elected to political office. They don't like bureaucratic hierarchy, but believe strongly in being recognized for their work on its creative merits. They especially believe in social diversity of all kinds, and feel comfortable working with others of different races or sexual orientations. Members of the creative class both work and play hard, and express only limited interest in accumulating material possessions and are especially oriented to consuming individual and shared "experiences" such as adventure travel, road biking or rock climbing or other vigorous activities, offbeat theater performances, cutting edge studio art, or experimental musical events. While Silicon Valley is a suburban bastion for such individuals, they increasingly find urban centers such as downtown San Francisco, Seattle, or Minneapolis to be exciting places to live and work.

Creative types, along with the return of aging suburban expats, fuel much of the boom in condominium construction and the conversion of distinctive older commercial buildings to residences in downtowns around the country. Both groups are attracted to the excitement of urban street life in neighborhoods with concentrations of trendy restaurants, theaters, art galleries, espresso shops, brew pubs, bookstores, and entertainment venues. Retailing matters, but its orientation is to specialty foods or wines, boutiques, and outdoor stores that serve the active life of the new inner city residents.

The interest of affluent young professionals in downtown living finds confirmation in a Brookings Institution study of census data by Eugenie Birch, Professor of City and Regional Planning at the University of Pennsylvania.[43] In a sample of 44 cities, downtown population grew by ten percent in the 1990s and the number of households expanded 13 percent, a substantial recovery after years of decline. In 2000 25 to 34 year olds compose a quarter of downtown populations, up from 13 percent 30 years earlier. The proportion of downtowners having a bachelor's degree rose to 44 percent, a figure that exceeds both that for cities as a whole and their suburbs. The young and the educated are exactly those groups where post-material values predominate.

Critics of this new post-industrial urban economy argue that the return of affluent residents to the inner city has done little to alleviate the poverty that prevails in many of its neighborhoods.[44] The aggregate economy of many central cities continues to sink despite renewed economic energy in their downtowns, and little progress has been made in revitalizing central city school systems. To have a shot in the long-run at entering affluent and creative occupations, inner city residents need education, and to survive and improve their condition in the short-run, they need job training and jobs. The presence of affluent professionals and empty nesters doubtlessly stimulate service sector employment and unskilled work in building rehab and construction, but without bolstering the minimum wage and improving access to decent health care, such jobs will not lead to much real economic progress among the inner city poor. In the longer haul, a strengthening of an affluent middle class who want to raise families in the inner city may create the political conditions necessary for central city educational reform to the benefit of all residents, but there is little evidence of this occurring as yet (Chicago is one among many cities making an attempt at serious educational reform). A concerted public effort to reduce climatic warming by switching to a clean energy economy and compact forms of living could bring a wide range of employment opportunities to central city residents in such fields as clean energy equipment fabrication, light rail construction, and commercial and residential energy conservation, but movement in this direction has stalled for now.[45]

Critics have also pointed out that Richard Florida's use of the term "creativity" to define a social class suffers from the problem of being too nebulous to be of much practical use.[46] Given the opportunity, almost anyone can exercise creativity in their work from the espresso barista who finds a unique way to pull a better shot, to a high-tech computerized machine tool operator who develops a new procedure for improving product quality, to a roofer who figures out a better technique for installing unobtrusive venting pleasing to the eye. It's not just an elite class of youthful software code writers, web designers, and graphic artists living in affluent downtown neighborhoods who are creative. So are the custom coffee roasters, microbrewery operators, gourmet bakers, and chocolatiers springing up in Milwaukee and most other central cities who often locate in rehabbed storefronts or old factory buildings. The rebirth of this kind of manufacturing in the central city occurs in those industries where the public increasingly demands the kind of quality and uniqueness large corporations are incapable of achieving. Creativity in the world of work need not be confine to a class of youthful professionals who value freedom, diversity, and self-expression. The aspiration and potentiality to be creative in some realm of one's life is a universal one unrestricted by occupation.

***

While the critics of a rising urban post-material professional class are right about a limited public concern with the problem of central city poverty, they have missed the trend to the rise of a modest income creative class as a driving force in the central city economy. Not all the creative occupations referred to by Florida in his writings enjoy the affluence of the creative class as a whole. True creativity doesn't necessarily bring wealth as the artists of the world have repeatedly discovered throughout history. Yet it is this group that concentrates most heavily among all occupations in the central city and serves as a driving force for neighborhood renewal.[47] The popular image of starving artists or aspiring actors as living in garrets and waiting tables for their living contains truthful elements. Artists, conceived broadly to include actors and directors, announcers, architects, drama and music teachers, authors, dancers, designers, musicians and composers, painters, sculptors, craft artists and printmakers, and photographers, are highly educated but poorly paid in comparison to other professionals. Artists often hold multiple jobs in a given year, work outside their chosen occupation to make ends meet, face frequent periods of unemployment, and contend with an income distribution highly skewed towards the relatively few who experience substantial success. Substantial financial accomplishment as a artist is a 'winner take all' gamble that very few attain. Nonetheless, the number of artists has has grown more than twice as fast as the labor force in recent decades, reflecting an expansion in public demand for the products and experiences artists have to offer as a well as a continued willingness of many artists to endure a lower income for the intrinsic rewards of creative work.[48]

Given their economic vulnerability, artists normally choose to locate in inner city neighborhoods with inexpensive rents. For those who require studios or places to rehearse, declining, seedy commercial or industrial areas often provide affordable space in which to both work and live. Artists concentrate in central cities to a greater degree than most other occupations and tend to cluster together in neighborhoods that best suit their needs for expansive but cheap workspace, community, and access to customers. Clustering enables interactions, from which spring ideas and information on economic opportunities, and the concentration of supporting art galleries and display spaces or performance venues. Over the last forty years, Chicago's Wicker Park neighborhood has evolved into what sociologist Richard Lloyd calls a "neo-bohemia" that originated in artistic clustering.[49] The neighborhood initially offered an abundance of old, unoccupied commercial space and working class bars that became outlets for performers as well as watering holes for invading "bohemians." By the late 1990s the neighborhood saw a growth of trendy restaurants, bars, entertainment venues, coffee shops, and art galleries popular with Chicago's growing class of young professionals. Along with this came a flood of building rehabs and condo construction pushing property values dramatically upward driving many of the artists that set off the whole process to cheaper rents on the neighborhood's periphery.

For Wicker Park, artistic vitality turned out to be self-destructive as it has for other so called bohemian communities such as Paris' Montmartre or Left Bank or San Francisco's North Beach. Post-materialist young professionals attracted to downtown living retain the consumerist ways of their affluent parents, but turn more to spending their dollars on shared experiences as opposed to the accumulation of material possessions, and they love doing so in a neo-bohemian bastion of creativity. They choose to live at high densities in condos and apartments for the privilege of participating in the varieties of human experience that requires proximity—music and entertainment, art galleries and public art, museums and the performance arts, and a lusty bar scene. Life on the streets and in the parks of a big city in itself constitutes a human drama that the suburbs are challenged to match. Part of the charm of neighborhoods like Wicker Park is their marginality and the oddballs and characters they attract. Suburbs are safe and convenient while the central city is dangerous but exciting and stimulating. The problem with the invasion of affluence into neighborhoods like Wicker Park is the pushing out of those people who create the bohemian ambience in the first place.[50]

While a neighborhood arts scene may be attractive to affluent consumers, gentrification need not be the inevitable result. Riverwest, a neighborhood with 11,500 residents just to the north of the Milwaukee's downtown described above, has evolved recently into a local arts and entertainment center with a growing collection of interesting bars and restaurants. The area was originally settled by working class immigrant Polish families more than a century ago who built modest duplexes and small simple frame houses. The neighborhood today also contains old store fronts and a number of aging factory buildings. Artists usually rent their dwellings, but one of the big attractions of Riverwest is the feasibility of purchasing a modest house or storefront that can serve as both a studio and a place to live. The humble character of the housing stock gives it an immunity from gentrification and keeps the neighborhood affordable and attractive not just to artists, but to a racially and ethically diverse collection of residents as well as students from nearby UWM. For the past twenty-seven years, the Riverwest Artists Association has sponsored ArtWalk, a walking tour displaying the creations of a hundred plus local artists at studios, galleries, and homes throughout the neighborhood, demonstrating the scale and endurance of the local arts community. If anyone expresses post-materialist values, it is artists, and alongside the arts community in Riverwest exist a number of activists groups with goals beyond material accomplishment, including the Riverwest Neighborhood Association, Peace Action Center, Riverwest Rainbow Alliance (an organization of gay, lesbian, bisexual, and transgender residents), and Children's Outing Association. While the occupants of expensive condos along the Milwaukee River on the southern edge of Riverwest may well be seeking post-materialist consumer experiences in the central city, the residents of Riverwest seem to hue even more closely to a post-materialist philosophy in their economic sacrifices for the sake of creative expression. Nonetheless, there is a certain economic symmetry in Riverwest's durability as an arts community and the springing up of affluent condo development nearby. Riverwest has artistic experiences and objects to sell, and the young professionals and suburban expats moving into nearby condos have the money to buy.[51]

***

The return of an affluent middle class to the central city in places like Chicago's Wicker Park and Milwaukee's Third Ward reflects a growing post-materialist interest in experiences that require a "shared consumption." When we share we get pulled outside of self-concern. This is especially the case with such events as musical performances, theatrical presentations, visual art displays, sporting events, and political pep rallies. In such instances, being a part of an audience or participatory group is an integral part of the experience. The same is true more casually in the enjoyment of a neighborhood's street or cafe life, or on a Sunday stroll through a park or along an urban lakeshore. In all such instances possession by the consumer is immaterial to the experience. Artists in central cities, who are themselves the paragons of post-materialist self-creation, acquire an economic niche by virtue of their ability to serve a post-materialist shift in the nature of middle class consumption. Artists survive by producing opportunities for experience. Post-materialist experience requires proximity, and compact living greases the skids of spatial proximity and promotes the sharing of experiences in both public and private spaces. It is in urban spaces where we get our fullest exposure to the diversity of the human experience, and where we have the greatest opportunity to submerge our personal egos in the content and flow of this larger reality. This is not to say that post-materialism lacks its dangers. The urban entertainment industry is driven partly by a dark Dionysian alcohol and drug fueled desire for ecstatic group experiences and sexual unions that can have exploitative and addictive outcomes, especially for those doing the work of serving (see the next chapter for more on this problem). Aspiring artists pushed into part-time service work out of economic necessity often have to put up with obnoxious and even violent behavior for the sake of getting tips, and can get stuck in doing work for much of their lives they didn't plan on. The post-materialist values of the young urban professional remain a mixture of hedonistic desire for urban entertainment and a self-transcendent interest in creativity and human diversity. Underlying this, nonetheless, lies a real passion for the products of human creativity. A Bohemia without creativity along with its lusty and tragic qualities wouldn't be much of a Bohemia. Artistic creativity ultimately produces objects and experiences that give insight into existential meaning. The post-materialism of young professionals may lack seriousness and for many may only be vicarious, but it does nonetheless support living more compactly in the service of human creativity.

Philosophy matters. For nearly a century now our human spatial dream has been materialist, spatially expansive, and suburban, but the winds of our dreams may now be subtly shifting toward a post-materialist philosophy and high density urban compactness that better serves post-material needs. We normally think of philosophy as something for academics to argue about, but it is more important than that. Our philosophical outlook lies behind how we live in the world, and a shift in the values by which we live can change the way we live.

A modest trend towards city living may not seem like much, but if it continues it will be a big deal. A shift to living at higher densities may well come in the nick of time to help reverse our ominous march to climatic warming. If you live in a densely packed central city instead of a spatially expansive suburb, you move around much less to get to work, for shopping, and doing all the other things you love to do. When you do move around in the city, chances are greater that you will walk, bike, or take public transit than if you lived in low density suburbs where odds are that you would drive everywhere because everything is so far apart. In short, if you move from suburb to city, you will cut back on your driving and the volume of auto-related greenhouse gas emissions you cause. Also in the city, chances are you will live in a smaller dwelling that requires much less greenhouse gas-emitting energy for heat and light, and if you live in a multi-family unit and share heat-emitting exterior walls and roof areas with others, your dwelling will be much more energy efficient than a single family, low rise house in the suburbs. By deciding to live in the city, you will do the environment a big favor whether you think much about it or not. If you are a post-material environmentalist, you might even decide to live in the city to live out your own philosophical values apart from realizing the benefits of city living. Again, philosophy is not just for the ivory tower but really matters in everyday life. A post-material future will differ from the materialist past.

Chapter 7: Jean-Paul Sartre's Existentialism and Starving Artists

Not everyone Richard Florida talks about in his book, *The Rise of the Creative Class,* are as lucky economically as he infers. The creative talent of Wicker Park described by Richard Lloyd in *Neo-Bohemia* struggle to make a living (as we just noted in the previous chapter), unlike their affluent young customers who haunt the neighborhood's galleries, espresso shops, and nightspots. It is in the Wicker Park bars and music venues that actual and aspiring artists and musicians work to make ends meet. In this hip, bohemian setting, servers, who treat their physical selves as their own vehicle for artistic expression, face special challenges daily. To gain and then retain their employment, servers must project a unique persona attractive to their experience-seeking clientele. Bar and restaurant owners compete for customers through the edgy image their establishments present. As Lloyd notes, servers have to strike a balance in the hustle for tips between pleasing their customers and fending off unwanted sexual advances. Servers also face the danger of getting caught up in the nightlife culture and neglecting their larger artistic goals, going out for free drinks on their nights off supplied by counterparts in other bars instead of doing creative work. Because these less fortunate members of the creative class face the kinds of dilemmas described by Jean-Paul Sartre's existentialist philosophy, spending a little time with his ideas should help us sharpen our thinking about the realities of a newly emergent "creative class" so important to the return to compact urban living.

In *Being and Nothingness,* Sartre begins by describing abstractly what it means to exist in the world. At a given moment we are an "in-itself," a simple object in the world like any other. As an in-itself we are no different than rocks, avocados, or snakes, or any other existent thing. But unlike non-human objects, we humans amazingly possess a consciousness with a capacity for self-recognition and reflection. Self-reflection brings forth a "for-itself" which constantly jumps ahead of what we are at any given moment (our in-itself) to think about our next move, our future actions. A constant restlessness puts us perpetually at the ready to move forward, to shift into a new and novel state of being. Here arise Sartre's notions of "not-being," negation, and nothingness. Never happy with our current condition, we keep pushing toward a desired future state. We don't have the house we want, haven't yet traveled to Australia or found the love of our life, and don't fully understand Martin Heidegger's philosophy much less Jean-Paul Sartre's. In short, we are never happy with what we are and press for something different. Our physical and mental in-itself is never up to our consciously wanted self-image. The in-itself is a thing in a certain physical state; consciousness is self-aware thought; and never the two shall meet. We live on a moving treadmill of not-yet-realized expectations from which we can never exit. We are not what we truly desire and are stuck in a special kind of nothingness—a not-being what we should.[52]

Sartre's basic premise is that existence lacks intrinsic meaning, and we are here in the world for no obvious reason. This fact gives us great freedom, intense anguish, and a huge responsibility. We have no alternative but to choose a path through life—we are "condemned to be free" as Sartre puts it. The life we choose is up to us and we bear the responsibility for how it turns out. Our fear that we will lack the courage to exercise our choice responsibly and authentically creates in us a deep anguish. Many of us try to avoid this by adopting roles and meanings in life that society coughs up for us, the tried and the true, the socially acceptable. Even then, subconscious doubt about what we should do and be will remain, causing us to continue in a vague and undefined state of anguish. If we go with the popular flow, we fall into a life of self-delusion and bad faith about who we are and really want to be.

Sartre has little use for bourgeois conformity and oppressive conventions, a view he expresses through the principle character, Rouquentin, in his best-selling first novel, *Nausea,* set in Bouville, a fictional commercial seaport on the French coast. While looking enviously on the fact that members of the Bouville middle class possess well defined life projects that supply them with a self-identity and meaning in the form of family, home, and profession, Rouquentin finds the repeated routines he observes in the life of the town as tedious and boring, even repellent. The presence of those nauseating others he observes around him with their socially determined projects forces Rouquentin to look honestly at his own life. He finds the historical research that he works on daily in the local library to be useless and comes to see the world around him as absurd and alienating and his own life to be an empty failure. The problem for him is an absence of meaning in his work, relationships with others, and the environment around him. Until the very end of the book, he can't see his way out. His conscious self doesn't know how to direct his being to a meaningful existence. Only in the final pages is there a glimmer of hope in his decision to move to Paris and write a novel (kind of like Sartre).[53]

The biggest pitfall we face in the quest for a life of meaning, Sartre tells us, is the danger of caving into society's demands for conformity and submission to social judgment. A lack of self-confidence in our own ability to choose a life-path causes us to look to our fellow human beings for acknowledgement, but we should do so with trepidation. Normal human affection—a relaxed and unthreatening felt connection to someone else—gets suppressed by the judgmental "look of the other," that "evil eye" projected on those who do wrong, calling for them to shrink in shame. The fear of social judgment holds out the danger of failing to be who we authentically want to be.

Consider the actions of a typical Parisian waiter as describe by Sartre in *Being and Nothingness.*

> His movement is quick and forward, a little too precise, a
> little too rapid. He comes toward the patron with a step a

little too quick. He bends forward a little too eagerly; his voice, his eyes express an interest a little too solicitous for the order of the customer...All his behavior seems to us a game.[54]

Sartre wrote this to illustrate the notion of "bad faith," the idea that we play at our role and do so to conform to practices demanded by the public. We get diverted by social requirements into adopting a pattern of life rather than creating one that is uniquely our own. We delude ourselves into thinking we act freely when in reality we succumb to the perceived judgment of others. In Sartre's eyes, social life boils down to an exploitive dance in which we fruitlessly try to control each others' perceptions. In the end, failure dooms us in such attempts. We can never really know our real influence on the true feelings of others. Rather than getting on with our own self-chosen authentic projects, in Sartre's view we waste our energies in the mutual pursuit of strategic and conflicting ends in our personal relationships. Whether he is right, I leave for you to judge. I can imagine other possibilities, such as something like the following.

Return for a moment to a Parisian café. Waiters follow traditional patterns in their work that comply with public expectations, but this does not rule out creative and unique interpretations of what it is to be a waiter. One can imagine a waiter doing his work in a way that authentically expresses his own idiosyncratic personality. A tall, handsome waiter of Haitian extraction glides to my table, inquires as to my well being, takes my order and magically appears moments later with my double café and croissant, placing them precisely and gently on the table while commenting on the beauty of the day. The man behaves with pride in his profession, something I can appreciate and enjoy. He spends time with each customer, some whom seem to be friends from the neighborhood who interact with him on a basis of equality and mutual respect. He later returns to collect my money, making change with dignity and efficiency. The next day I return for a repeat performance. This time a customer, who is elegantly dressed, looks wealthy, and probably comes regularly, sits down in the cafe several minutes after me. The waiter, aware of the circumstances, serves me first despite the obvious impatience of the snooty regular. This is what a good waiter does as a matter of practice, refraining from any strategic judgment about ultimate rewards in deciding who to serve first. We don't see the whole of our Haitian waiter in our brief interactions, but we do see at least part of his life that seems to honestly express who he is.

One could take this alternative interpretation of a waiter's life too far. No occupation is an entirely a thorn-free bed of roses. Customers can be difficult, muscles will ache after a long day, and repetitious tasks can be tedious. Still, one sees pride in the affectations of at least some waiters who indeed perform for us, but who do so with authenticity and real concern. Participating creatively in the tradition of a Parisian waiter could be a consciously and freely chosen activity, much like writing *Being and Nothingness*. The question for us here is whether the freedoms in behavior enjoyed by our Haitian waiter, or for that matter of a book-writing Jean-Paul Sartre, extends to the artists and servers of Wicker Park.

The heyday of arts community predominance in Wicker Park occurred in the 1990s prior to an influx of young, affluent professionals into the area. A few of the bars were already emerging as entertainment venues for rock bands who attracted outsiders into the neighborhood, but most of the cafes and watering holes were oriented to a local clientele. By 2000, the neighborhood had become a cultural and entertainment destination with and expanding array of restaurants, bars, galleries, antique stores, and boutiques depending largely on a youngish, affluent clientele. At this point developers became active in the area constructing new housing for upper income customers. While rising rents pushed some artists to the neighborhood's periphery, the area retains its bohemian and hip flavor even though the local population mix has shifted decidedly in favor of those who work in Chicago's downtown business establishment. Digitally tuned-in local artistic talents has attracted a number of web design firms who require not only computer literacy but an aesthetic sensibility in their employees as well.[55]

Wicker Park retains a class divide between young professionals and artists that finds its clearest expression in the neighborhood's bars that rely heavily on an influx of affluent youths seeking a Bacchanalian ecstatic experienced fueled by music, drink, drugs, and a potential for sexual liaison. The primary source of labor for local bars and restaurants is the nearby arts community whose members depend on such work for a living while pursuing entry into their chosen careers. Youth, looks, and a unique, hip fashion sense help immeasurably in getting hired as a server or bar tender in Wicker Park. Unlike the conformity to tradition of Sartre's Parisian waiter, Wicker Park servers are rewarded for an offbeat and unique style in their appearance which becomes a design element for bars and nightclubs in their competitive efforts to attract customers. Servers in this environment enjoy the opportunity of expressing their own artistic skill by creating themselves as a work of art. The downside in this form of expression is the role it plays in competition for both employment and tips. Female servers must balance success as a server and the extra tips that can come with a sexually provocative look against the problem of unwanted sexual advances from male customers. In short, the capacity for creating a unique style is limited by the expectations of not only bar owners but tip-supplying customers as well. Just as is the case for a Parisian waiter, the work of being a Wicker Park server can be strenuous, repetitive, and at times boring. Servers also have to deal with social pressures from their colleagues to go out drinking in their off hours, taking away time from their artistic pursuits and downtime from the physical and mental stresses of the job. Alcohol addiction and a failure to pursuit professional goals can be the end result. As one server expresses it, "If I'm still here in a year, kill me."[56]

The artistic quest can be an authentic and laudable pursuit of expressions of meaning that help to "spiritualize" the Dionysian love of life talked about by Friedrich Nietzsche in *The Birth of Tragedy*. The visual and performance arts possess the capacity to help us both celebrate and sublimate life's powerful sensual urges that can easily get out of control. Artists serve us by providing an opportunity to find and sacralize meaning in the experience of life, rather than the in the heavens beyond. If anyone can overcome the dangers of Sartre's bad faith and anguish in choosing a path through life, artists have a good chance at it. As we see for Wicker Park servers, circumstances can nonetheless conspire against them in obtaining their hearts' desires. While they may see themselves as uniquely creative individuals, the conditions servers face can work against them in truly attaining their artistic purposes. They face a special danger of exercising a self-delusive "bad faith" by ignoring their true condition.

Whether or not the Wicker Park case constitutes a widespread phenomenon matters. If artists create urban communities that ultimately get destroyed in a gentrification process driven by an influx of post-materialist young professionals, then this new form of compact living will possess a dark and undesirable quality. While many well known urban bohemian districts have succumbed to affluence, all arts-based neighborhoods needn't suffer the same fate. Milwaukee, a seemingly ordinary older industrial city, surprisingly contains a substantial population of artists, many of whom have taken up residence in inner city neighborhoods such as Riverwest and Bayview. As already describe earlier, Riverwest houses numerous artists, art studios, interesting restaurants and bars, and a variety of entertainment venues, including the Jazz Gallery run by the Riverwest Artists Association. Riverwest serves as a local bastion of activist, left-leaning politics that attracts substantial involvement by local artists and adds a stabilizing element to the neighborhood. Despite a solid core of artists living and working in the neighborhood and an expanding nightlife, unlike Wicker Park, Riverwest has avoided an influx of affluent young professionals into the neighborhood and a surge in property values. Artists have been able to solidify their presence by taking up ownership of aging, affordable Polish flats, duplexes, and storefronts that have little middle class appeal but can be rendered into comfortable and pleasing spaces in which to live and work. The local nightlife lacks the supercharged energy of Wicker Park, but provides a more community oriented and less exploitive working environment for servers and bartenders most of whom live in the local neighborhood just like many of their customers.[57]

The experience of other cities confirm the reality of two divergent paths for the impact of the arts on urban neighborhoods. In those first tier artistic centers such as New York and San Francisco, concentrations of artists in neighborhoods often become attractors for development of the type experienced in Chicago's Wicker Park. In cities where housing pressures are less substantial such as Philadelphia or Minneapolis-St. Paul, researchers find that artists often bring neighborhood revitalization of the kind we see in Milwaukee's Riverwest without much displacement of ethnic or racial minorities. Artists in these cities find urban havens with an immunity to high pressure gentrification where they engage in a political activism that helps to stabilize the neighborhoods in which they settle. In sum, the growth of the arts profession nationally has led to local creations of moderate income but stable compact urban communities. It's not just the return to the central city of affluent professionals that drives an urban renaissance. The social and economic dynamic of a Riverwest appears to be more friendly than a Wicker Park in overcoming the anguish and tendency to bad faith we all face in making something of our lives. The kind of post-materialism we see taking shape in the Riverwests of the urban world as opposed to the Wicker Parks may well help us surmount the barriers to an authentic human existence raised in the philosophy of Jean-Paul Sartre and celebrate the wonders of humanity and nature emphasized in the philosophy of both Friedrich Nietzsche and Martin Heidegger. Again, we see that the philosophy of life actually possessed by

individuals matters for the unfolding of the future in the real
world.

Chapter 8: Post-materialism and Work

To repeat one more time, meaning in life comes from adopting and pursuing purposes about which we care passionately. For most of us a substantial portion of our waking being is taken up with paid work, something we must do in order to earn an income to supply the material instruments of life. If meaning comes from materialist ends, then the purpose of work would be to make money and all else wouldn't matter. While earning an income is the predominant motive for working, the activity of work serves more functions than just a means to material existence.

For many of us, work is the social center of our lives. One of the most robust findings of happiness research is the importance of friendships for life satisfaction, and it's at work where we develop many of our enduring friendships that spill over into our life as a whole. Work can provide more than just money and friends if we are lucky. Truly interesting work challenges our intellectual and physical abilities and causes us to enter into a state of active engagement—what psychologists call flow—where immediate feeling-state concerns evaporate. During the activity of such work, consciousness of pleasure or pain disappears, and it is only after the fact that a warm glow of satisfaction and accomplishment emerges. To top it off, work holds out the possibility of achieving those creative purposes that bring meaning to our life. It is not just the activity of work that matters to us, but the final purpose it serves as well. Of course not all work provides a full range of such benefits. Much work is tedious and boring, offers only limited opportunities for social interactions, and lacks a valued purpose. In such instances, work is undertaken for narrower ends. One could imagine a highly skilled hedge fund manager making millions of dollars but secretly believes the purpose of the work to be trivial or even socially destructive, or a poorly paid nursing home aide who finds the work itself to be tedious and stressful but believes it to be of high social importance.[58]

The non-economic dimensions of work take on a special importance for post-materialist young professionals. They desire work that allows them to creatively apply their talents and skills to socially valuable undertakings and they want to do this in a socially interesting environment. The recently established General Assembly, a Manhattan incubator for web application and service businesses, fills the post-materialist bill for code-writing entrepreneurs who rent glassed-off office space abutting a common room where tenants can enjoy a cup of gourmet coffee while chatting with their fellow digital pioneers about their latest web successes and failures. A recent startup, Yipit, an aggregator and analyzer of daily internet commerce deals, began by renting space in the General Assembly, but after successfully generating revenue flows for its services, moved to its own home in nearby office space, Ping-Pong table included.[59] We don't normally think of New York City as a high technology paradise, but it now trails only San Francisco as a haven for digital startup capital. The blending of work and leisure in New York's new high tech culture is evident in the new "techie fashion shows, techie reality TV shows, techie entrepreneurs on the Council of Foreign Relations, and techie scalpers hawking tickets outside the New York Tech Meetup, the industry's premier (and perennially sold-out) monthly event." New York's "Silicon Alley" flourishes in part because of the decline of Wall Street as an attractive career path and the desire to avoid being a cog in a bureaucratic wheel and returning to the tradition of "craft work" where the final product of one's efforts can be directly observed.

Such a vision of work in the new technology world may not apply universally. Zynga, a highly successful internet gaming startup, warranted a *New York Times* article with the title, "Zynga's Tough Culture Risks a Talent Drain."[60] Frustrated workers complain about long hours, stressful deadlines, and a relentless tracking of progress and performance. Those who don't measure up are quickly shown the door. The esprit de corp common to many internet companies has been replace at Zygna with an intense individualistic meritocracy, but without a serious dent in the company's economic success. While Zynga may be an outlier in its extreme methods of work organization, intense internal competition amongst employees tends to prevail in the gaming industry. Apparently there is more than one way to skin the high technology organization cat. Not all startups fulfill post-materialist workplace desires.

Research for industrialized countries on how people feel about their working life finds that most are satisfied with their jobs, but that satisfaction is higher where the work is interesting and good relations with management prevail. Opportunities for working independently and good pay also play a role in work satisfaction but fall below the first two factors in importance.[61] These statistical results provide backup for what Richard Florida (*The Rise of the Creative* Class) finds anecdotally in focus group conversations with "creative class" post-materialist young professionals. Post-materialists want in their work what most of us want—a degree of control, social connection, engaging activity, a sense of accomplishment, and a worthy purpose.[62]

Despite feeling satisfied with their work, some Americans are unhappy about the amount of hours in a year they actually spend on the job. About 37 percent want to work fewer hours, around 22 percent want to work more, and the rest are content with their time on the job. High incomes and a college education results in a preference for reduced working hours, contrary to anecdotal reports of creative class satisfaction with long hours.[63] Young people at Google and places like it may be happy with periods of long work hours in a fun work environment, but they are unlikely to want this for the whole of their working lives. The statistical reality is that a post-materialist attachment to the quality of work itself leads to a desire for fewer hours, while unsurprisingly a belief in the importance of earning a high income results in a desire to work more hours. Materialists want more hours, post-materialist want fewer. Liking work doesn't necessarily mean you want long days on the job.

The one odd quirk in American work time preference studies occurs for working families. Working parents, who more than others face a time-bind in their daily lives due to family responsibilities, ironically desire more hours on the job. One explanation is simple and compelling—a need for higher income to meet the costs of raising a family. Another explanation is a little unexpected—a desire to escape the impositions of family existence. Despite our love for children, parental life satisfaction declines during the child rearing years according to happiness researchers.[64] While we love our children, work at times can be a respite from the challenges of parenting.

A comparison of the U.S. and European experience with work offers up a more deeply puzzling result about American work time desires. Europeans and Americans worked about the same number of hours in a week per person back in the 1970s, but since then the hours worked has declined dramatically in Europe but not in the U.S. Today the French and Germans work about three-fourths of the average annual hours of Americans. About a fourth of these lower hours derive from a shorter normal workweek and the rest from a combination of more holiday and vacation days and lower workforce participation. While real income growth follows a comparable path in the U.S. and Europe, Europeans have chosen to take economic gains in the form of fewer working hours and more leisure while Americans have not.[65]

Surveys find that Europeans experienced an increase in life satisfaction as their hours work decline. By contrast the more Americans work, the proportion reporting themselves to be "very happy" rises slightly, while the more Europeans work, such a report declines markedly. Europeans clearly prefer to work fewer hours and spend more time seeking their satisfactions elsewhere. Americans by contrast find happiness in working more hours rather than fewer. Europeans place more value on the quality of work than Americans, while Americans value the economic results of work more than Europeans. Europeans apparently tradeoff the satisfactions of work against those of leisure while Americans balance the virtues of leisure against earned income. Income wins out for Americans and leisure for Europeans. As one researcher puts it, "Americans live to work while Europeans work to live."[66]

In looking at the data on post-materialist values, one would think Americans would be just like Europeans in their working-time desires. The proportion of Americans holding post-materialist values sits in the same ballpark as Europeans. Why don't Americans more strongly express their post-materialism in a preference for fewer working hours more on the order of Europeans? While some Americans want to work less, the majority are either content with their working hours or want to work more. This is a puzzle precisely because of a comparable prevalence of post-materialist values in both the U.S. and Europe. The answer to this puzzle may well lie in the ironclad connection between employment and access to health insurance in the U.S.

A key barrier to shorter hours in the U.S. economy not found in Europe is the way in which health insurance is delivered. In most European countries health insurance coverage is universal and funded largely through government. In the U.S. health insurance for most is tied to full-time employment and the cost is partially funded by employers as a benefit. The very poor receive health insurance from the government through Medicaid and the elderly from Medicare. Because American employers provide very limited health insurance benefits to part-time workers, many would prefer to have full-time work simply to obtain health insurance at a reasonable cost. Buying health insurance in the U.S. on one's own is a costly proposition. Given that health insurance benefit costs vary with the number of workers and not average hours worked, employers can often save money by hiring fewer workers at longer weekly hours to meet a given product demand. In short, the U.S. health insurance system creates a bias towards a longer average workweek and against part-time jobs with health insurance benefits. In Europe, part-time work can be chosen without sacrificing access to health insurance because its availability is assured by government, but in the U.S. few part-time jobs offer affordable health insurance.[67]

The health insurance issue takes on special importance for a key subgroup of the creative class, the starving artists. Many artists are self-employed in the U.S. and lack access to affordable health insurance. Many also supplement their income from part-time work that lacks health insurance benefits. The health insurance problem forces many American would-be artists to seek full-time work in other fields. Because European artists don't need to worry about health insurance costs, they experience greater flexibility than Americans in combining their artistic efforts with other kinds of work to supplement their incomes.[68]   Anyone who truly wants to work part time in the U.S. will be forced to contend with low pay and a lack of health insurance.

As the Dutch have demonstrated over the past 30 years, part-time work needn't be marginalized and relegated to a lower economic status than full-time work. The Dutch have adopted government policies that require equalized hourly pay and access to benefits for equivalent part-time and full-time work. Dutch workers also have a right to request reductions in their individual working hours with proportionate reductions in pay. Since the introduction of these reforms, the share of part-time work in the Dutch economy has increase dramatically and the hours worked per capita has decline significantly as well. The share of part-time employment in the Netherlands exceeds that for all other European countries, and the Dutch seem to be perfectly happy working less than others. Unlike American part-time workers, very few Dutch desire a shift to full-time employment. All this has been accomplished alongside employment growth and declines in unemployment.[69]

The U.S. has considerable distance to go before equalizing the status of full- and part-time work, but, with the recent passage of the Affordable Health Care Act, part-time work in the future will look somewhat more attractive to Americans. Beginning in 2014 under the Act, anyone will be able to acquire health insurance policies on government-run exchanges without having to worry about denial for pre-existing medical conditions. Because the cost of such policies are to be subsidized for those with limited incomes, obtaining affordable health insurance coverage as a part-time worker will be much easier. The new health insurance reforms will benefit artists and others who seek satisfaction of their creative impulses outside of conventional full-time work and desire part-time employment to help satisfy their material needs.

Affordable health insurance will increase the appeal of lower paid but more creative work, and this will in turn increase the attractiveness of compact urban neighborhoods for those who choose to pursue a post-materialist path to meaning. If full-time work is required for health insurance, then the higher income that comes with it will make a spatially expansive, consumption-oriented life in the suburbs feasible. If one makes a bundle in less than fully satisfying employment, then you might as well spend it on the pleasures of a comfortable house and the convenience of a luxury motor vehicle. But if conventional full-time work is no longer needed for health insurance, and the pursuit of one's true passion becomes possible through less remunerative activities, then the likelihood of a turn to a more affordable way of life in a spatially compact setting will increase. We have already laid out key post-materialist attractions of high density urban living such as access to lively neighborhoods, entertainment and the arts, good cuisine, and interesting architecture, but for those on a limited budget other features matter as well such as the ability to find affordable housing, use public instead of private transportation, and substitute public for private space. Life in compact cities is lived more in public arenas, such as parks, squares, libraries, and coffee houses, instead of in spacious suburban houses and big backyards. Entry to public spaces normally costs little while the ownership of private space can be costly. Getting around densely packed cities by mass transit, on foot, or by bike is often more convenient and certainly less expensive than by motor vehicle. Post-materialism as a way of life is available not just to affluent young professionals in urban centers, but, as artists have demonstrated, for those willing to give up income in order to satisfy deeply held creative urges and values. Artists and others who seek a less materially oriented way of living have been at the forefront of carving out an affordable urban niche by revitalizing deteriorated, older central city neighborhoods. If one doesn't have to face excessive costs for access to health care, then the adoption of a truly post-materialist form of life will be significantly eased and compact living will be given a boost.

Those free spirits who desire to follow their own idiosyncratic passions in life will have their path eased by such government interventions as the Affordable Healthcare Act. Even the ultimate free spirit, Friedrich Nietzsche, who hated the centralized German state of his day, might well have appreciated the idea of government provided universal access to health care, especially given all his physical maladies.

Chapter 9: Post-material Values and the Turn to Vegetarianism

Middle Eastern restaurants seem to be all the rage in Paris, London, New York, and almost any other European or American city. We in the affluent West have taken a shine to pitas, hummus, falafel, kebabs, stuffed grape leaves, yogurt sauces, and vegetable stews with eggplant, pine nuts, olives, squash, peppers, and a variety of wonderful spices. Shifting toward a Middle Eastern diet would not only be a tasty thing to do, it would be good for our health and a benefit to the environment.

We in the U.S. consume a bit more than 3,800 calories a day per person of which a whopping 900 come from animal products. This figure is unadjusted for spoilage, waste, and loss in food preparation, meaning that the actual U.S. average daily calorie intake is more like 2,700.[70] The recommended healthy calorie intake for a moderately active adult male is about 2,400 with no more than 10 percent coming from protein. Clearly, we Americans consume much more meat than we need and way too many calories. Nearly 24 percent of our calories come from meat protein alone, well above the 10 percent recommended amount. No wonder we face an epidemic of obesity. The developed countries of the world as a whole including N. America and Europe, don't do much better in achieving a healthy diet, with an average daily calorie consumption of 3,600 of which 750 comes from animal products. Japan is the only affluent country in the world that comes anywhere near a healthy diet at 2,700 per capita daily calories consumed with 350 from meat products. Despite discouraging statistics on calorie intakes from most affluent countries of the world, we needn't necessarily despair about solving the global obesity epidemic. A variety of time-tested, tasty global cuisines that are good for us are available from all over the world including Japan, Vietnam, Thailand, Africa, Latin America and the Middle East. An abundance of calories and large intakes of animal-based protein isn't essential to the pleasures of eating.

Consider what would happen if we in the U.S. adopted a Middle Eastern diet or one comparable to it. Our daily calorie consumption would drop to around 3,300 with about 300-400 coming from meat. Our calorie intake would then be on par with Turkey and Saudi Arabia, both of which are fairly affluent, and a bit above Tunisia, a developing country. We Americans could accomplish parity with a Middle Eastern diet simply by cutting our meat consumption in half. Doing so would not only bring substantial health benefits, but would also amount to a huge favor for the environment.[71]

The essential environmental problem with meat flows from the large amount of land and energy required to grow animal feed grains.[72] To produce a gram of animal protein in the developed countries requires about 10 grams of vegetable protein. Because our extraordinary intake of animal protein in the U.S., we devote half our farmland to animal protein production for just 24 percent of our calories. If we cut our meat consumption in half and move toward a "Middle Eastern" calorie standard, we could cut our agriculture land for animal products in half, reducing our total land devoted to agriculture by a fourth. This would leave a substantial chunk of land available for natural habitat restoration, renewable energy production, or other uses. Feed grains, especially corn, require a massive amount of fossil fuel energy to cultivate, not only to run farm equipment, but for producing the large volumes of nitrogen fertilizer and pesticides applied to fields and crops. A hectare of corn uses up the amount of energy equivalent to that in 230 gallons of gas, and emits an equivalent of 4 metric tons of CO_2 annually. Cutting corn production by a quarter in this country (about half is currently devoted to animal feed) alone would reduce our CO_2 emissions by approximately 30 million metric tons per year. A second substantial environmental benefit from growing less corn would be reductions in fertilizer runoff from Midwestern corn fields that end up in the Gulf of Mexico causing a "dead zone" that appears annually from fertilizer-induced oxygen depletion.[73]

To sum up, the citizens of North Africa and the Middle East use much less land and energy than we westerners do for food and have a healthier diet as a result. In short, their food production system is much more compact than our own, directly by using less land, and indirectly by absorbing less fossil fuel energy. Is there any chance at all that dietary patterns in the U.S. and Europe will move in a Middle Eastern "vegetarian" direction in the future to the benefit of both human health and the environment? The trend to post-materialist values offers some hope on this question.

We have already talked about how a post-materialist trend increases compact living in cities and reduces fossil fuel energy consumption, both of which have substantial affects on the amount of global space left over from human use for the rest of the world's flora and fauna. The single biggest human use of land in the world today is for agriculture. If we adopt a healthier, less animal-protein oriented diet, we will need less land for our food, and can leave more for nature. If post-materialists are less inclined to animal-based protein consumption, then over time the global diet will become more spatially compact. The question is, are post-materialists more likely than others to move in the future towards a vegetarian cuisine?

About five percent of the U.S. population defines itself as vegetarian according to a recent Gallup Poll.[74] While we don't know the proportion of post-materialists that follow a vegetarian diet, researchers have studies the value foundations of vegetarianism pretty carefully, suggesting that we can establish whether vegetarianism and post-materialism intersect. Vegetarians are more strongly oriented to environmental protection, altruism, self-direction, and stimulation than omnivores, and omnivores possess values more strongly oriented to tradition, conformity, and security than vegetarians. Recall that post-materialists give substantial support to protecting the global environment, advancing the well-being of all humanity, and free self-expression. Post-materialists also savor visual and esthetic stimulations, something that a tasty interesting cuisine can provide, and lack much interest in tradition, conformity, and security, values supported by omnivores.[75] In short, post-materialist value orientations differ little from vegetarians. In their food choices, vegetarians take into account ecological and health effects to a greater degree than omnivores and essentially see their dietary practices as a way to realize concretely their basic philosophical orientation. Food is about much more than just the pleasure of eating for vegetarians, and since vegetarians philosophically are for all intents and purposes post-materialists, one can reasonably hypothesize that a growth in post-materialism will bring forth more vegetarians. Vegetarianism is one way post-materialists can effectively live out their values. While the data on vegetarianism is insufficient to statistically tie its presence to post-materialism, there is good circumstantial evidence backing the hypothesis. If the link is substantiated, then growth in post-materialism will mean expanding vegetarianism which will in turn lead to more human compactness, less climate change, and more space for nature.

Chapter 10: Philosophy Matters for Climate Change

Philosophical outlooks held by actual people make a difference in their daily economic lives. As we have seen here, the shape of our global future is moving steadily into the hands of post-materialists who downplay narrowly economic goals in favor of self-expression, personal autonomy, and a universalist concern for the well being of both humanity and the nature. Will attitudes post-materialists express towards the problem of climate change truly matter for the future? Can the clout of a politically powerful, entrenched minority of climate change deniers be overcome by a growing popular majority deeply worried about the consequences of global warming for the earth's environment? Taking a careful look at what we know about actual human attitudes on global warming should help us all form a better judgment about where our climate future is headed.

Post-materialists support for environmental improvement manifests itself both directly and inadvertently. Direct support includes choosing to live in an energy efficient dwelling for the conscious purpose of reducing carbon emissions, or voting for a senate candidate who promises to work for legislation that will limit climate change. Inadvertent support results from choices undertaken by post-materialists for purposes other than environmental improvement. A software engineer, who sells her 5,000 square foot house in Silicon Valley and gives up her job at Google in favor of a 1,000 square foot apartment in San Francisco in walking distance of her new job at a startup working on educational software for inner city students, unintentionally reduces her carbon emissions footprint by living more compactly. We already know that post-materialists lead an economic resurgence taking place in compact older urban areas around the country, a trend that reduces energy consumption and carbon emissions as a side effect. In focusing less on material accumulation and more on qualitative experience in daily life, post-materialists unintentionally do the environment a favor.

Post-materialist impacts on the global environment turn out to be more than unintentional. We will now empirically tie down the link between post-materialism and direct support for environmental protection and climate stabilization. What do researchers know about the relationship between post-materialist values and concern for the environment and climate change, and how do they know what they know?

Social scientists investigate relationships between demographic, environmental, and attitudinal variables using a range of survey research and statistical techniques. In studies of human values and the environment, researchers draw on large statistical samples for their basic data such as the World Values Survey, covering 50 countries and asking respondents a variety of questions about their lives and personal attitudes and beliefs, or the International Social Survey program's 2000 module on the Environment conducted in 26 countries on topics related to environmental concern. A commonly applied approach for sorting out relationships among variables is regression analysis, a procedure that determines whether a dependent variable is affected statistically by hypothesized independent variables. Surveys, for example, ask respondents about the degree of their concern about climate change, or their willingness to pay more taxes to improve environmental quality, and the extent to which they hold post-materialist and other sorts of values or beliefs. Using such survey results, researchers employ regression analysis to test whether respondent environmental concern is statistically affected by post-materialist values, various other attitudes, and demographic characteristics such as age and income. In this way, the effect of post-materialism on environmental concern can be estimated holding other independent variables constant.

    Richard Englehart, the leading chronicler of the global
trend to post-materialist values, published a paper back in
1995 suggesting that post-materialists express greater
support for environmental protection than others. To make
his case, he used simple bar graphs of survey data on
post-material values and support for the environment
without engaging in extensive statistical tests.[76] Since
then, a number of more detailed statistical studies confirm
the positive connection between individual environmental
concern and post-materialism.[77] This is the case both for
general expressions of environmental concern and more
specific worries about climate change, as well expressions
in the form of willingness to pay added taxes for funding
environmental improvement or reducing climate change.
Post-materialists above all support human self-expression
and individual freedom, but they also want a quality global
environment.
    While post-materialism is important, researchers find
evidence for other determinants of environmental concern
as well, such as how it is positively affected by educational
attainment and specific knowledge about the environment.
Not just values but knowledge matters, both in the form of
general educational achievement and a detailed
awareness of environmental issues. Beyond these, being a
women or relatively young results in more intense
expressions of environmental concern, although one study
finds environmental concern to be greatest for middle-aged
respondents. Similarly, personal actions to improve the
environment, such as recycling or green political action,
intensifies environmental concern just as does a liberal
political orientation. In countries at earlier stages of
economic development, conservatives and liberals
surprisingly both express strong concern about
environmental degradation, but as an economy matures
and becomes more capitalist, and as the most serious
environmental problems are addressed in response to
political pressure from a growing middle class,
conservatives lose their worries about the environment and
become rigorously oriented to economic expansion as a

primary social goal, environment be damned.[78] This is quite an amazing result about the environment and politics suggesting that liberals and conservatives find common ground in the right circumstances. But once an economy achieves a threshold of affluence and a modicum of control over the most gregarious pollution problems, business coalitions against environmental regulation form to retard environmental improvement in favor of unhindered economic expansion, a phenomenon very apparent in the U.S. over the last fifty years. Here liberals and conservatives part company. American political conservatives today are among the staunchest climate change deniers and liberals the most intense believers, except of course for scientists who have the highest belief level of all. To summarize our findings so far, concern for the environment depends positively on post-materialist values, education, being young, being a woman, specific knowledge of the issue, and a liberal political orientation.

Climate change as a problem possesses unique features that sharply distinguishes it from other environmental issues. Unlike air pollution in the form of smoke or ground level ozone or water pollution in lakes and rivers, the effects of climate change lack direct visibility. We can't see carbon emissions, and we can't trace natural disasters such as Hurricane Katrina directly and unambiguously to climatic warming. Climate change, as real as it is, remains an abstract hypothesis and requires special science-based knowledge to be understood. Affluent countries such as the United States have made substantial progress in addressing visible pollution, but not so much for climatic warming. Unlike most other pollution problems, climate change is global in scope and results from greenhouse gas emissions no matter where they occur. The contribution of any but the largest and wealthiest countries to greenhouse gas emissions is such a small part of the total, that individual actions by most countries to curtail emissions would have little impact on the problem as a whole. In the absence of a globally coordinated approach to limiting greenhouse gases, no single country has much incentive to do anything about the problem. Climate change thus requires combined action by all countries for real effectiveness, a deeply challenging prospect.

Nonetheless, apart from the U.S. and a few other high-emission countries, modest progress has been made in addressing climate change through the 1997 Kyoto Protocol. Countries to jump on the Kyoto bandwagon first with an early treaty approval possessed certain features: Already relatively high ratios of GDP to energy consumed and low rates of greenhouse emissions per capita; relatively high levels of educational achievement; well developed democratic institutions; and a record of cooperation with other countries on global issues.[79] One would expect less of a challenge for countries in meeting Kyoto emissions reduction targets if they already possessed high rates of energy efficiency per unit of GDP and if they already had relatively low levels of CO_2 emissions per capita, and countries with these two features were indeed predominant among the early approvers of the Kyoto Protocol. One would also expect that a national commitment to education and political democracy would matter as well for early Kyoto approval as would the possession of a "universalist" orientation to global cooperation. In contrast to early approvers, the U.S., with its extraordinary levels of per capita fossil fuel energy consumption, faced greater costs than many countries in reducing emissions. Substantial political opposition to the Kyoto Protocol in Congress by the fossil fuel lobby and business interests led to its defeat in the treaty approval process.

Without the approval of the Kyoto Protocol by the U.S., the European Union became the backbone of the treaty among the world's largest greenhouse gas emitters. The original fifteen EU member nations unanimously approved the treaty and collectively adopted centrally regulated greenhouse gas emissions reductions and tradable emission allowances.

A post-Kyoto Protocol survey in the EU shows strong citizen support for their region-wide system of environmental regulation, especially among the original fifteen member-states. As in many studies of environmental attitudes, the degree of post-materialist values held by EU respondents positively affects their willingness to sacrifice income for the environment. Also, as is typically found in other studies, younger EU respondents and political liberals lend greater support than others to spending money on environmental improvement. A positive impact of GDP per capita on willingness to pay for environmental improvement across all countries of the EU supports the idea that more income leads to a greater demand for environmental quality and an enlarged capacity to pay for it.[80] As one would expect, a lesser degree of support for EU environmental regulation is expressed by citizens of less-wealthy Eastern European member nations that joined the EU later.[81] To sum up, post-materialism, youth, education, and economic prosperity matter for support of environmental improvement in the EU.

These results for the EU do not mean that worries about the environment and climate change are confined to just the affluent countries of the world. A recent study of 47 countries, including both rich and poor, using the latest World Values Survey finds the following: Concern about global warming is unchanging across countries with higher and lower GDP and CO_2 emissions per capita; concern is positively affected by post-materialism, a leftwing political orientation, religious involvement, and education level; concern is negatively affected by being a male respondent, having a rightwing political orientation, and experiencing weather-related natural disasters; and middle-aged respondents express greater concern for global warming than either older or younger ones.[82]

None of these relationships is too surprising except for the negative effect of weather-related natural disasters. Disasters cause a decrease in concern about climate change among respondents, contrary to expectations. One would think that exposure to a climate related disaster would increase respondent climate concerns, but for many the link between weather and climate change may not be well understood. As a practical matter, those recently affected by such disasters may have immediate problems that pushes climate change down their list of worries. Figuring out how to recover from a flood today for many no doubt takes precedence over concerns with the uncertain future effects of climate change.

The lack of a positive relationship between concern for climate change and income across rich and poor countries together makes more sense for a global problem such as climate change than it does for a local problem such as ozone pollution. At a local level, prosperity brings with it greater demands for improvements in environmental quality, as noted above. At a global level, low income countries will bear the brunt of climate change costs in the form of drought or flooding, and it is the high-income countries of the world who possess most responsibility for future climatic warming. Given this reality, equal concern about climate change between low- and high-income countries looks less surprising. Wealthy nations may well face a demand for climate stabilization related to income, but it is the poor of the world that will experience the full force of climate change damage. The poor of the world face the indignity of a problem foisted on them by the rich, and it is the rich that have the primary responsibly for cleaning it up. If anything in these circumstances, the world's poor should be expressing more concern about climate change than the rich, and we will now see that in at least one survey they do.

Two economists recently used the International Social Survey program's 26-country 2000 module on the environment to tease out the effects of respondent attitudes and other factors on the perceived seriousness of global warming and the ultimate impact of such perceptions on actual greenhouse gas emissions.[83] What drives climate concerns among citizens, and do such concerns matter for government actions on climate change? Based on a large sample of individuals in the 26 countries, the researchers find the perceived seriousness of greenhouse warming to be influenced at statistically significant levels as follows: Positively by respondent affinity for the global community and support for public goods in general and long-term public goods in particular (such as climatic stability); positively by educational attainment, liberal political affiliation, and urban residency; and negatively by a lack of familiarity with the climate change issue, respondent age, and per capita income.

In earlier chapters we talked about "universalist" values that include a general concern for the well-being of humanity as a whole and for the natural environment in general, and we noted that post-materialists tend to be universalists. The statistical results just summarized suggest that universalists values in the form of global affinity, support for public goods, and a liberal political orientation positively impact the perceived serious ness of climate change. This infers that post-materialism would have a similar impact were it included in the study since post-materialists tend to be universalists. Because of its lack of direct visibility, knowledge of the climate change issue matters for judging its seriousness, and statistical evidence indicates this to be the case. Finally, the impact of income on the perceived seriousness of climate change is negative, supporting the idea that low-income respondents express greater concern because they are the ones who bear relatively greater harm from the problem and less responsibility for it.

A huge challenge for all of us globally is to bring climate change to a halt and to bring global temperatures back to levels that no longer pose a threat to life on earth. The philosophy we possess affects the values we have, and our task here is to set out how in practice values matter for what we do in the world. We now know that post-materialist and universalist values along with lower per capita national income, greater educational attainment, and a liberal political outlook make a difference globally in beliefs about the seriousness of climate change. The question to be addressed is simple: Do such beliefs matter for climate change itself? Let's take a look at research on just this question.

Countries with relatively low actual growth of greenhouse gas emissions possess the following: A more extensive belief among their citizens that climate change is a serious issue; a greater the degree of press freedom; greater citizen trust of government information on pollution; and the absence of either very high or very low per capita GDP levels relative to the average. What do these research results mean for the impact of philosophy and values on real world actions? In a democracy responsive to citizen concerns, we would expect worries about climate change to be reflected in government actions to limit greenhouse gases, and the findings tell us that they do. The greater the proportion of citizens in a country who believe that greenhouse warming is dangerous for the environment, the lower the pace of growth in greenhouse gas emissions, inferring that governments must be taking action to limit emissions. The curtailing of such emissions is augmented by press freedom, which brings greater awareness to the public about issues of importance such as climate change, and by public trust in government information about the environment. Finally, whether a country is wealthy or poor doesn't play a role in the determination of actual practice for limiting greenhouse gas emissions, suggesting that cross-country income differences operate through citizen concern about the environment and not apart from it. As already noted, individual citizen worries about climate change are negatively affected by income.

The essential take away message here is that citizen attitudes matter in limiting greenhouse gas emissions. With a rising proportion of post-materialists in the global population who favor doing something about climate change, actual results look to be on the horizon. Countries whose citizens express concern about climate change have done more than others historically to limit their greenhouse emission growth. The question remains whether post-materialist political influence will be strong enough in the future to fully offset the incredible power of vested fossil fuel economic and political interests, especially in the United States. To this issue we now turn.

***

U.S. environmental survey respondents have the special distinction of expressing a below average concern with climate change, a below average knowledge of the subject, and a below average trust in government information on the environment.[84] These survey findings help to explain why the U.S. in the last two decades failed to sign onto the Kyoto Protocol and adopt regulatory limitations on greenhouse gas emissions.

An environmentalist transported by a time machine from the late 1960s and early 1970s to the present day would be surprised and shocked by a lack of U.S. action on climate change. With the election of President Obama in 2008, expectations were high that Congress would past a cap and trade bill placing limits on overall greenhouse gas emissions. A proposed bill was to accomplish this through a system of emission allowances that would shrink in number slowly over a thirty-five year period. These allowances were to be bought and sold in a market that would permit emitters with high control costs to buy allowances from those with low costs, reducing the economic burden of forestalling climate change. The House of Representatives passed such a bill, but the Senate never approved it.

To the President's credit, his administration has dramatically tightened future fuel efficiency standards for motor vehicles that bite deeply into carbon emissions, invested government funds in clean energy businesses, offered subsidies for investments in carbon-free energy production, and started the process of regulating greenhouse gases from utilities and industry under the Clean Air Act. In the meantime, industry interests and conservative groups have mounted a substantial lobbying and public relations campaign against greenhouse gas regulation, including attempts to discredit scientific studies on the relationship between burning fossil fuels and climate warming, an effort that seems to have paid off by suppressing public climate change worries.

Environmental politics differed substantially back in the early 1970s when such legislative landmarks as the Clean Air Act, Clean Water Act, and Endangered Species Act were passed by Congress and signed into law by a Republican President, Richard M. Nixon. In those days, environmental issues ranked high in public concern, and the environmental movement looked invincible. Industry lobbyists seemed impotent in the face of a well-organized and popular effort to mitigate a variety of harms to the country's natural environment. The success of environmentalism began its long decline with a series of economic crises in the mid-1970s and early 1980s initiated by the 1973 Arab oil embargo undertaken to punish the U.S. for its support of Israel in the Yon Kippur War. Even though the embargo ended, world oil prices continued a dramatic rise with the creation of the OPEC oil cartel and its success at limiting world oil supplies. This turn of events caused global economic havoc including runaway inflation and a double-dip recession in the U.S. deeply serious economic problems caused by the energy crisis served to strengthen opposition to environmental regulation, and business interests mounted a successful campaign of opposition both in the courts and Congress against implementation of environmental legislation by the Environmental Protection Agency. Life for the environmental movement toughened further with a conservative turn in national politics ushered in by the ascendency of Ronald Reagan to the presidency in 1980.

It was not until the passage of the 1990 Clean Air Act Amendments in the first Bush administration that the environmental movement experienced any success at all in the legislative arena. the 1990 Amendments created a cap and trade system for sulphur dioxide emissions implicated in the problem of acid rain causing serious harm to pristine lakes and forests in the northeastern U.S. Although the 1990 Amendments were successfully implemented at below expected costs to the public, the U.S. environmental movement has achieved little since, especially in bringing greenhouse gases under control despite accumulating scientific evidence of the link between emissions and climatic warming and the extent of both projected and already accruing harms.[85]

While both the U.S. and Europe exhibit comparable trends in the growth of post-materialist values, European environmental concerns and actions on limiting climate change outpace those in the U.S. Based on the rise of post-materialism, the U.S. and Europe should have similar trends in environmental concerns and accomplishments, but they don't, at least in the last two decades. Because of its greater energy intensity brought on by a more spatially expansive and auto-oriented way of life, the fossil fuel industry is relatively larger in this country than Europe, and fossil fuels constitute a powerful economic interest with a well-honed political capacity to oppose greenhouse gas emissions regulation. The motor vehicle industry once was in the same political boat as fossil fuels, but this is less the case now with the necessity of the recent federal bailout to save the industry from extinction. Hardly a peep arose from the auto industry with the imposition of increased fuel efficiency standards by the Obama administration.

Despite environmentalism's political setbacks in the U.S., there is room for hope in the future. The continuation of the post-materialist trend will slowly but inexorably raise the average level public concern for both the local and global environment if past behavior as documented by researchers holds true. Post-materialists will also continue to adopt a more compact, energy-efficient form of urban life that will serve as a drag on fossil fuel demand. Finally, there are good reasons for governments to impose a price on greenhouse emissions, either through an emissions tax on or a cap and trade system, as we will now explain. Philosophy will matter in the form of a trend to post-materialism, but economic trends will matter as well in the curtailing of fossil fuel consumption and greenhouse gas emissions.

***

Let's begin with the short story on the economics of clean energy, solar and wind especially, and energy conservation. (For the long story, see my *The Coming Good Boom*).[86] Energy conservation, the simple act of using less, turns out to be a "free lunch" in the eyes of most experts. Over the next forty years, we can reduce our consumption of energy per capita by about a third at zero net cost. This means that cost savings pay for the investment required to achieve a third less energy consumption through such measures as buying hybrids and other fuel efficient motor vehicles, adding insulation to our attics, installing energy efficient lighting, living in more compact and energy efficient buildings, and expanding mass transit systems.

On top of efficiency gains, to get unhooked from carbon-based energy, we will still have to come up with the other two thirds of our current energy consumption, and if we want to bring climate change to a screeching halt, this will have to be from zero greenhouse emission sources such as wind, solar, biofuels, and nuclear. Because of public opposition, expanding nuclear power beyond current levels can probably be ruled out, leaving us with wind, solar, biofuels and a variety of sources with a smaller potential such as geothermal and various kinds of waterpower including small scale hydro and tidal.[87] Biofuels, such as ethanol from corn, haven't been very promising so far because energy inputs into their production exceed the energy available in the output. The future does look brighter for biofuel from agriculture and other kinds of waste with progress being made on the technology of converting plant materials containing cellulose to ethanol and garbage to hydrogen. Assuming an energy system based on solar and wind, in forty years our inflation adjusted energy bill might be 10-15 percent higher than it is today, but since our real incomes are likely to rise much more than this because of labor productivity gains (each of us producing more stuff), the relative energy bill burden will actually decline.[88] Wind is already closing in the on the current cost of energy from coal, and solar will do the same within the next twenty years according to Energy Department projections.

Such cost reductions have as their source a standard economic phenomena—the more you produce of something, the lower its average cost. This idea of "scale economies" will make solving the problem of climate change less costly, but it also presents a critical barrier to transforming our energy system. Right now electrical generating volumes for wind and solar are insufficient to compete with coal and natural gas, but if they were scaled-up, their unit costs would fall. Fossil fuels unfairly get a free ride on the external costs they cause from global climate change damage. If a prices were imposed per ton for greenhouse gas emissions that accounted for such costs, fossil fuel prices would rise relative to clean energy and investment in wind and solar would expand, causing their unit costs to decline at an accelerated pace as scale economies kick in.

Economists suggest two alternatives for getting climate change costs incorporated into fossil fuel prices: a tax on emissions or a cap and trade system. Either one places a price on greenhouse gas emissions that fossil fuel producers must pay. The scientific clearing house for climate change research, the Intergovernmental Panel on Climate Change (IPCC), suggests that a $100 per ton global price on carbon emissions (and their equivalents in terms of climate change potential) will be needed by 2030 to put a lid on climatic warming. Assuming that such a cost is fully passed onto the consumer, the result would be about a dollar increase in the price per gallon of gasoline and an $.10 increase per kilowatt of electrical energy generated from coal. Such increases would cause coal to be much more expensive as a source of electrical energy than either wind or solar, and give a boost to biofuel and electric powered motor vehicles. If the $100 price increase per ton of emissions were spread out over 15 years, this would amount to less than a penny increase per kilowatt of coal-fired electricity and $.07 increase per gallon of gas annually. Everyone would have plenty of time to adjust to energy price increases by shifting to wind and solar power, more energy efficient housing and appliances, and high-mileage motor vehicles that run on clean energy. Because the current boom in natural gas has driven the cost of gas-powered electricity generation below coal-fired plants, the life of carbon-based energy will be extended under a carbon pricing regime, but since the carbon content of natural gas per unit energy is only about half that of coal, greenhouse emissions will still be reduced. Eventually carbon-free energy will be cheaper than even natural gas according to Energy Department projections as the price of carbon emissions rise over time.

In comparing the virtues of cap trade to a carbon tax, there isn't really much to argue about. A carbon tax of $100 would directly fix the price of emitting a ton of carbon, and the volume of emissions would be determined by the decisions of energy consumers. The basic idea is that consumers would reduce their use of increasingly expensive fossil fuels and expand their consumption of relatively less costly untaxed clean energy. Under cap and trade, the government would fix an annual emissions limit for each of the next forty years that would in the end drive emissions to near zero . In each year issue emission allowances for the volumes allowed within the caps would be issued to emitters. These allowances could either be auctioned off by government or given away and their price would be established by market forces. Auctioning would create a new source of government revenue comparable to collecting a tax. Over a twenty year period the revenue collected in the U.S. could amount as much as $4 trillion and could be used to put a substantial dent in our national debt currently running around $16 trillion. If the $100 price by 2030 is enough to do the work of capping global warming, then a tax and cap and trade are essentially equivalent. In the first instance, government sets the price per ton of carbon and in the second instance it sets the volume of emissions allowed. The tax is conceptually simpler, but allowances assure that emissions caps are realized and give industries more flexibility in meeting their limits. Personally, I am agnostic on the two approaches; either will do the trick.

An attractive feature in the current political climate for putting a price on greenhouse emissions is its revenue generating potential to use in reducing the national debt in a manner that increases the burden on consumers very slowly. Even more attractive is the ability for consumers to avoid much of the price on carbon through improving their personal energy efficiency and by switching to clean energy sources, something that would be infeasible if the debt were paid down through higher taxes on incomes tough to avoid.

A second attractive feature of a greenhouse emissions price is its potential for stimulating an economic boom based on the creation of a new clean energy industry. An essential economic virtue of clean energy is its ability to generate employment. Both wind and solar require a wide range of employee skills for design, installation, maintenance, and operations, and the volume of employment needed per unit of energy is much higher for solar and wind energy than it is for fossil fuels. Studies estimate that the production of electricity from either coal or natural gas requires an average of 0.11 person years of labor per gigawatt hour of power, while solar photovoltaics use and average of 0.87 person years and wind 0.17 person years per gigawatt hour.[89] These numbers are calculated over the typical lifespan of energy production facilities and account for labor employed in design, installation, maintenance, and operations. Clearly, clean energy is much more labor intensive than fossil fuels, and converting energy supply from fossil fuels to clean energy will add jobs to the economy. The same is the case for reducing energy consumption through energy efficiency measures adding about .38 person years to employment per gigawatt hour of energy saved. A study summarizing these findings suggests that meeting growth in energy demand completely from energy efficiency measures combined with 30 percent of electrical energy coming from clean sources in 2030 will add 4 million jobs per year to the economy net of reductions in fossil fuels. Scaling this up to a totally green energy electrical economy, would multiply this number to more than 12 million jobs. Right now 60 percent of energy consumed occurs outside of the electricity sector in motor vehicle and other types of transportation, dwellings, industries, commercial establishments, and agriculture.[90] In a clean energy economy, an expanding share of total energy consumed will come from electricity as opposed to solid or liquid fuels, meaning that net employment gains by 2050 will be even more than our projected 12 million jobs. Liquid fuels from biomass will require about twice as much employment per unit energy as natural gas, suggesting that even if we stick to liquid fuels for powering our transportation system, clean fuels will stimulate more jobs on net than the fossil fuels they replace. Besides biofuels, a second potential huge gaseous fuel source is hydrogen produced from electricity, stimulating a further expansion in electricity sector employment. Hydrogen in turn can be used to power fuel cells in motor vehicles and elsewhere that provide a mobile and flexible source of electrical energy.

Placing a price on carbon will have the immediate impact of telling everyone that the days of fossil fuels are numbered, and that money is to be made instead in clean energy. This will spark an immediate boom in the design and installation of clean energy capacity and a front-loading of employment in solar, wind, and biofuels. There will be some employment leakage to imports, as has been the case recently for low-end solar panels, but the research and design as well as installation portion of employment will be predominantly a local affair and will constitutes the vast bulk jobs created in solar energy. Given the scale and bulk of wind generating equipment, manufacture and assembly will normally take place close to the site, and the same will be the case for large-scale thermal solar facilities springing up in desert landscapes in the U.S. and elsewhere. Biofuels production will be tied to the waste sources they depend on. A surge in clean energy will be accompanied by added employment growth in energy conservation work as well, such as upgrading heating and lighting systems and insulating older residences and commercial buildings. With rising fuel costs, the construction of energy efficient light rail lines will look increasingly attractive as an alternative to the automobile for getting around. Light rail expansion will also have the side benefit of accelerating the trend to compact living by increasing the ease of living in high density walkable neighborhoods near transit lines. Taxes are normally thought of as a depressant to economic expansion, but a tax on greenhouse emissions will set off an economic boom driven by clean energy. This boom will in turn create diverse new employment opportunities across a wide range of skills helping to resolve challenging unemployment problems, especially in older, denser cities suited to compact, energy efficient living.

Politicians in the future will have increasing difficulty ignoring the growing clout of politically active post-materialists who will be an expanding share of the voting population and who already express deep concern about climate change and environmental decline. A greenhouse gas emissions tax will gain in political popularity not only as a virtuous environmental and boom-creating economic measure, but as one with the special side benefit of raising tax revenues over the long haul and bringing down the level of government debt. What could be better? Once these virtues of clean energy are fully recognized, the power of the currently formidable fossil fuel lobby will look much less imposing. Philosophy in the form of a growing post-materialism will turn out to matter along with the virtues of clean energy economics in finding our path to a better future.

Chapter 11: What Philosophy for the Future? Getting along with Islam

My personal impression is that philosophy, much like theology, or even cosmology, until recently has been on a quest for an explanation of everything, of Being itself. This explanation takes form as a final cause, something uncaused that causes all else; in short, a god-like force of some kind. For most of us, who seek principles to live by that help us get from one day to the next, figuring out the beginning of all causal chains, the ultimate mother of all beings, seems like a tough row to hoe unlikely to bear many fruits of real value. Some modern philosophers seem to agree, and focus their writings more centrally on phenomenon in the perceivable world. Our discussion of post-materialism follows in this vein. Some post-materialists express concern about the larger existential questions, but they usually place these within a private spirituality as opposed to an established, "final cause" oriented, religion that offers its own explanations about the source of all being and provides its own principles to live by. In short, post-materialists are more entrepreneurial and pragmatic in creating their own philosophies for guidance through life. Although post-materialism is on the rise in the world today, it has yet to attain predominance as a source of human values. The reality is that majorities in many countries of the world follow traditional religious practice for their philosophy to live by. While post-materialism will play a role in guiding the world as a whole into the future, it will continue to share that world with traditional religions expressing faith in a final godly cause of all else.

Our innate human tendency is to be philosophically tribalistic rather than express a universalist concern for the fate of the world as a whole. A tribalist will care for the community and place of their immediate being while a universalist will also feel an affinity for beings beyond their tribal boundary. The attachment to tribe seems to originate in evolutionary processes and genetic interest while a larger concern for all beings seems rooted in consciousness and holistic reflection that takes one beyond immediate genetic interest. Consciousness creates self-awareness that no doubt has an evolutionary advantage but also brings forth worries about the finiteness of being and personal significance in the course of natural and historical events. Here we have to cope with our inability to verify metaphysical proposition about final causality through observation and reason, and we get into the dangerous and unsettling position of having to accept faith-based explanations for existence or look elsewhere for life's meaning.

One pragmatic and simple solution is to worry less about the why of Being and to focus on how interesting and amazing it is irrespective of its final cause, godly or otherwise. We can then get on with everyday life comforted by the wonder of all that surounds us. Once we take a closer look, amazements are everywhere, and experiencing and understanding our little corner of being ought to suffice in keeping us excited about our existential world. Don't worry too much about metaphysical origins; focus instead on self-creation within the cultural and natural hand you are dealt. This is a modern pragmatic solution to the mystery of Being that post-materialists might find appealing.

Yet life is more than just self-creation. It is social and ecological, and we have to worry about placing our self-creativity in a larger context. Richard Rorty makes an interesting distinction between the public world where we decide on justice and fair treatment and the private where we pursue our particular self-creative path. But the trouble comes if self-creativity is bound up with the public treatment of something internalized in private identity. Rorty claims that the worst thing we do is treat others with cruelty, and it is up to us to act publicly to diminish the amount of cruelty in the world. The rub comes in deciding what kind of cruelties belong in the public arena. What about the developer of a privately owned property who destroys a patch of rare orchids, a cruel act for nature lovers, a group that at one time included Rorty himself who in his youth became a self-educated expert on orchids? Should such cruelties be subject to public concern? Private self-creativity can spill over into the public realm, instigating in a democracy a continuous political dialogue and struggle on where the boundary lies between private and public. This is especially the case when different cultures possess different outlooks on the distinction between public and private.[91]

A post-materialist philosophy supports taking a public path to a future green and clean economy in the first world, but what about the more tradition-oriented and less affluent third world? Why would poor countries want to take seriously the problem of climate change when they have more immediate worries, such as famine and poverty? First world post-materialists want to bring climate change into the global public arena, but why would a tradition-oriented citizen of the third world be interested? Why, for instance, should a low income North African country such as Egypt care much about climate change in light of its other economic and social woes? Given the power of tradition in countries like Egypt, can a post-materialist trend play any role at all in bringing about a green and prosperous Middle East rooted in a commitment to limiting climate change? Is there a common ground between traditionalists and post-materialists in constructing a philosophy for the future in this part of the world?

One place to look for answers to such questions is simple material interest. Scientists were recently predicting up to a meter climate change induced rise in sea level by the end of this century, but now some have changed their tune. With melt rates for the Greenland and Antarctic Ice sheets greater than anticipated, experts now believe that sea-level will increase 1-3 meters by 2100 and 5 meters if ice-sheet breakups takes place. The effects of a 1 meter increase will be challenging, but 5 meters could be catastrophic. Those countries that will suffer the most from climate caused sea-level increases are low-lying, such as the Bahamas, and possess extensive river deltas, such as Viet Nam, Egypt, and Bangladesh. Population displacements, declines in gross domestic product, and a loss of land area from inundations of croplands, urban landscapes, and wetlands will be commonplace. The hardest hit country from a 1 meter sea-level rise will be Viet Nam with projected inundation of 5 percent of its total land area, 7 percent of its agricultural lands, 11 percent of its urban extent, and nearly 30 percent of its wetlands. Egypt, is second only to Viet Nam in projected potential damage from sea level increases. While Egypt won't loose much of its 1,000,000 square kilometer mainly desert surface area, with its population and arable lands so heavily concentrated in the Nile River Delta, even a meter sea-level rise will be devastating. From such an increase, Egypt will see some 13 percent of its 40,000 square kilometers of cropland inundated, and as much as 9 percent of its population will suffer displacement. A 5 meter sea-level rise would increase the cropland loss to 35 percent. For the likes of Egypt, climate change constitutes a huge long-term material worry.[92]

Ironically, solving the problem of climate change will bring huge economic benefits to Egypt. Abundant and cheap clean energy is globally essential to solving the world's climate problem, and Egypt is well placed to bring clean energy to a significant chunk of the world's population from its extensive sunny, hot desert landscapes. In order to both gain an economic benefit and avoid a substantial harm, informed Egyptians out of self-interest will want to see the climate change problem high on the global public agenda.

Apart from a straight forward analysis of gains and losses, where would a heavily traditional country like Egypt come down on environmental issues generally, and climate change in particular? Can religious conservatives also be environmental radicals? An Egyptian commitment to the Muslim faith puts us in a philosophical arena distinct from what we have described so far. Post-materialism takes an agnostic position regarding questions of final cause and focuses predominantly on how collectively and individually to best get through life. Religions, such as Islam, instead profess God to be the creator of all things and the final source of daily principles for the faithful to live by. As we will now see, recent survey research offers interesting insights into the different value commitments expressed by respondents in countries with a traditional religious commitment and those with a secular and post-materialist orientation.

In its coverage, the World Values Survey allows researchers to place countries surveyed on two separate spectrums: first, traditional versus secular/rationalistic values, and second, economic security versus self-expression values. Countries with respondents who predominantly claim the following fall on the traditional end of the first spectrum:

> God is very important in their life; children ought to be taught obedience and religious faith as opposed to independence and personal autonomy; abortion is never justified; national pride is important; and authority ought to be respected.

Countries whose respondents predominantly express the opposite of these beliefs fall at the secular/rationalistic end of the first spectrum.

Similarly, countries with respondents who predominantly claim the following fall at the economic security end of the second spectrum:

> That economic and physical security take precedence over self-expression and the quality of life; that they are not very happy with their lives; that they never have and would not sign a petition; that homosexuality is never justified; and that one has to be careful about trusting people and countries.

Respondents who predominantly express the opposite of these beliefs fall on the self-expression end of the spectrum. Muslim country respondents, including Egypt, tend on average to fall at the traditional end of the first spectrum and the economic security end of the second. Western European country respondents tend towards the secular/rationalist end of the first spectrum and the self-expression end of the second. The U.S. ranks high on self-expression, but surprisingly toward the traditional end of the tradition-secular/rationalistic spectrum. In short, the U.S. combines a traditional orientation with high post-materialism.[93]

While Egyptians as a whole are strongly oriented to traditional values and economic security, those born since 1960 exhibit greater support for self-expression than everyone else, and do so with increasing margins at younger ages. Although a concern for material security rules today in the Muslim world, the desire for self-expression by younger generations is on the rise suggesting a slow but inexorable future shift over time in favor of post-materialism.[94] Post-materialism, with its emphasis on free self-expression, remains a weak force in Egyptian society, but it seems to be growing among the young. A growing demand for self-expression by Egypt's youth appears to be an underlying motivation for the Egyptian Arab Spring revolution sparked by young tech-savvy activists able to use cell phones and the internet to organize protests against the Mubarak regime. The revolution achieved its goal of getting rid of dictatorial rule, but the organizational capacity of the tradition-oriented Muslim Brotherhood with the backing of a Muslim majority has won the day so far in gaining governmental power in Egypt. Demands for self-expression got the revolutionary ball rolling, but the show is now in traditionalist hands.

Given the power of their commitment to traditional Islam, it is not a little surprising that survey respondents in Muslim countries, including Egypt, express extraordinary levels of support for political democracy regardless of the intensity of their religious involvement.[95] Survey researchers find globally that a prevalence of self-expression values precedes the success of political democracy[96], but Egyptians seems to be putting the democracy cart before the self-expression horse. In the World Values Survey as just noted, Egyptians worry more about economic security than self-expression, but

Egyptians of all ages seem willing to follow the lead of the country's youth in bringing about a democratic revolution.

Young and old alike in Egypt agree that government has historically failed miserably in both aiding the country's poor and addressing serious environmental problems that plague Cairo and other areas. Belief in the obligation for Egyptian society to addressed both these issues can be traced to basic Muslim doctrines such as the Koranic requirement of care for the less fortunate, the Islamic call for cleanliness in daily life, and the deep Islamic reverence for all of God's creation including the world of nature. A common ground on problems facing Egypt among a liberalizing youth and their more religiously devout elders may well be enough to bring together citizens of all ages in support of democracy. A survey of Egyptians on the environment finds that those with a strong religious commitment actually express greater concern about environmental degradation than others.[97] Young post-materialist Egyptians and their religiously devout elders appear to have a common interest in mitigating the countries serious environmental problems.

Egypt's move to democracy is by no means problem-free. Serious political tensions are already evident because a majority of older, more religious Egyptians want a democratic government to support traditional Muslim values including restrictions on gender equality and homosexuality. Young and old agree on democracy, economic justice, and environmental improvement, but Egypt's self-expressive youth demand greater gender equity and protections for individual freedoms than a Muslim majority may be willing to grant. In short, Muslim majorities in the Middle East are in a state of rebellion against ineffective dictatorships that don't serve anyone's interests other than ruling elites, but the ultimate position that democratic majorities will take on questions of personal freedom and self-expression remains to be seen. Successful democracy in the rest of the world bears a strong relationship to a level of gender equity that conservative Muslims may not yet willingly allow.

While Egyptian post-materialists and traditionalists differ in their basic philosophical commitments, they do have a common interest in doing something about global environmental decline. Egypt's traditional Muslim values when applied to the environment lead to practical concerns not that far afield from those of post-materialists. Add to this the real threat posed by climate change to the agriculturally rich and densely populated Nile Delta, Egyptian worries about environmental issues are well founded. (Recall from the previous chapter that low-income country residents express a stronger concern about climate change than their more affluent counterparts in some surveys.) A global movement to a clean and green economy also offers substantial potential for Egypt's future material development to the benefit of both young post-materialists and older traditionalists. An essential element in bringing about an Egyptian green economy will be an internal capacity for social invention and innovation needed to put the country on a positive path to the future. For this to happen the following question will require an answer: can a free-wheeling entrepreneurial commitment to new solutions for social and environmental problems that fits best with a post-materialist philosophy in the end also be compatible with a commitment to Islam? Stay tuned.

Chapter 12: Post-material Social Invention in Egypt and Tunisia

Making as much profit as possible defines the essential motivation of a capitalist and materialist economy. Only those economic innovations that bring significant profits will be of interest to materialistic capitalists. In a post-materialist world, the motivation for innovation broadens. Profitability continues to be important, but innovation takes on a social dimension as well. Post-materialist innovators possess a broader array of social goals in the work that they do than profit alone. We get a hint of this in the Sergey Brin and Larry Page experience of founding Google. They went into business because they wanted to create the best possible internet search engine. Of course they made an incredible amount of money along the way and its hard to discount the motive of profit in their case.

The idea of social innovation has gained a special currency among academic researchers in recent years who have begun to take a serious look at the driving forces behind what has come to be known as "social entrepreneurship." The notion of "entrepreneurship" has been around for a very long time and refers to the act of creating and running a new business enterprise that delivers a good or a service for the purpose of making a profit. The notion of social entrepreneurship refers to the act of creating and running a new organization with a goal of accomplishing a social purpose. Both the founders of Google and Facebook have publicly expressed social goals for their organizations, although, again, profit cannot be dismissed in these two instances as a driving force.

Survey researchers work to identify concretely the phenomenon of social entrepreneurship with a question that takes the following form: "Are you, alone or with others, currently trying to start or currently owning and managing any kind of activity, organization or initiative that has a particularly social, environmental or community objective?" A second question ascertains whether a survey respondent is involved in starting a for profit enterprise: "Are you, alone or with others, currently trying to start a new business or owning and managing a company, including any self-employment or selling any goods or services to others?" Respondents answering the first question positively are "social entrepreneurs" while respondents answering the second question positively are "commercial entrepreneurs." In cases where the same respondent reports a positive response to both questions, a third question is asked to determine if the businesses referred to in the two responses are one in the same, and the overlap counts as a social business. Across an adult population survey sample of from 49 countries at different stages of economic development, the incidence of early stage social entrepreneurialism (an organization that is 3.5 years old or less) ranges from a high of 4.1 percent in the United Arab Emirates to a low of .1 percent in Guatemala. The rate for the U.S. is comparatively high at 3.9 percent. The global average is 1.8 percent with low income countries averaging 1.3 percent, middle income 1.8 percent, and high income countries 1.9 percent. The incidence of total early state entrepreneurialism by country, including both social and commercial, averages 10.7 percent with the respective figures for low, middle, and high income countries equalling 16.9, 11.3, and 6.6.[98]

Given what we know about post-materialist and materialist human motivations, we would expect post-materialists to be attracted with greater frequency than materialists to socially oriented entrepreneurship. Cross-country survey research on commercial entrepreneurialism finds that it correlates negatively with post-materialism, inferring that a reduced desire for economic achievement dampens profit-oriented business formation. This research also finds that the ratio of social to total entrepreneurialism across countries is positively correlated with a country's incidence of post-material values. Where post-materialism is relatively strong, so is social entrepreneurship. A country's per capita income positively correlates as well with the ratio of social to total entrepreneurialism. Wealth, post-materialism, and social entrepreneurship all move together.[99]

Poor countries, such as Egypt, who lack a robust corporate sector, out of economic necessity possess a large sector of small, new businesses, many of which are found in the "underground" economy. Everywhere in Cairo, Egypt someone is trying to sell something. For many of the city's residents, small enterprises provide the only path to earning a living, and not very many of these can afford to pursue a social mission. Nonetheless, social enterprises exist in Egypt and other low income countries. Remember, the incidence of early stage social entrepreneurs in poor countries average a non-trivial 1.3 percent in comparison to the 1.8 global average. Social entrepreneurship indeed occurs in low income countries, and its incidence rises as development takes place along with growth in post-materialism.

To give on-the-ground content to social entrepreneurialism, we will now look at specific cases for Egypt and Tunisia demonstrating the potential of post-material social invention in fostering what I have called a "good boom," an economic expansion that lifts all economic boats and takes on previously intractable social and environmental problems. Along the way we will discover agreement on certain key human purposes between an emerging post-materialism and a more traditional Islamic philosophical orientation. Modern liberal Islamic scholars argue that to accept such values as environmentalism, gender equity, democracy, and self-expression, one can still adhere to a Muslim heritage. The acceptance of the Koran, with its poetic descriptions of worldly being as God's creation, needn't run against a modern commitment to personal freedom, economic justice, self-expression, and saving the environment. We will leave the theological justification for this view to others and focus instead on examples of its real world manifestation.

***

Ibrahim Abouleish grew up in a Cairo neighborhood in the 1940s and 1950s where many Jewish families lived, attended a Christian school, and became deeply attached to his Muslim faith at an early age. He attended university in Austria where he obtained a medical degree as well as training in research chemistry. After completing his studies, he embarked on a successful career in pharmacological research in Austria, married an Austrian, and started a family. He took a special interest in the study of philosophy, especially the works of Rudolph Steiner, which he used to read and interpret the Koran in what he considered to be a spiritually more insightful fashion. Dr. Abouleish enjoyed and admired European culture but remained a committed Muslim throughout his life. Unlike many other Egyptians, Dr. Abouleish expressed opposition to war with Israel in the 1960s.[100]

Although he returned to Egypt frequently to visit his family, Dr. Abouleish did not travel extensively in the country until 1975 when he took an eye-opening trip with an Austrian friend. He was shocked by the catastrophic degradation of agriculture in the Nile Valley and the physical decline of Cairo and its living conditions. Construction of the Aswan High Dam in his eyes was an unmitigated disaster by halting the age-old annual flooding of the Nile that covered fields with life-giving fertile mud. Farmers were forced to compensate for this loss of fertility by applying large amounts of fertilizer which led to excessive salting and soil compression.

On his return to Austria, Dr. Abouleish further investigated and pondered what had happened to Egypt and began to seek alternatives to the continued degradation of the rural landscape. He became especially interested in biodynamic agriculture, a type of organic farming developed by students of Rudolph Steiner's anthroposophy. This form of farming had been successfully applied for decades in Europe, especially in Italy. After traveling and learning about biodynamic methods, Dr. Abouleish set aside his research career and, with his wife and children, moved back to Egypt in 1977 to establish an organic farm. The farm became the focal point for the Sekem initiative, the name of which was adapted from ancient Egyptian hieroglyphics for the life-giving vitality of the sun.

Sekem, headquartered at the original farm site north of Cairo, includes five different companies that employ 1,800 people and produce and distribute a variety of organic products including natural medicines, cereals, rice, vegetables, pasta, honey, jams, dates, spices, herbs, edible oils, herbal teas, juices, coffee, milk, eggs, beef, sheep, chicken, seeds, and organic cotton textiles and clothing. One company, ISIS, distributes more than 80 percent of the herbal teas sold in Egypt. Sekem currently operates five farms on reclaimed desert lands that provide almost a third of the company's organic raw materials and has created permanent "Fair Trade" ties with small farmers for the rest. Sekem's secret weapon in desert reclamation is compost, a product it both uses itself and sells to other farmers. Compost rich soil in deserts increases fertility and productivity, retains much more water than conventional farm soil (essential in an arid climate), and sequesters substantial amount of carbon in its accumulated organic matter.

While Sekem is a profitable venture, its goals and activities extend well beyond those of a conventional business. Sekem has successfully advanced its founding vision of creating ecologically sustainable oases in the desert where health-giving organic goods can be grown in a manner protective of both the local and global environment. In and around these oases, Sekem seeks to create communities where individuals can not only improve their material condition, but expand their educational and culture capabilities as well. In all its efforts, Sekem adheres to strict standards for the protection of human rights (including religious freedom), achievement of gender equity, and educational and cultural advancement as well as rigorous targets for environmental sustainability including carbon emissions reduction.

Through its Development Foundation, Sekem established a school located on its headquarters farm serving 300 kindergarten, primary, and secondary students. The students come from a diversity of social backgrounds, including both Muslims and Christians, and the school emphasizes respect for all religions and contains both a mosque and chapel. In addition to following the Egyptian state curriculum, the school makes a special effort to provide courses in crafts, drama, dance, and music. Sekem has its own orchestra that performs in the local community and gives special support to the practice of Eurythmy, a dance form originating in Europe. The Foundation has also established a modern medical center nearby that serves 120 patients or more a day from employee families and the local community. The clinic offers a variety of outreach programs that address such issues as women's health, family planning, and sanitation. In addition to these efforts, the Foundation also offers vocational training and education in organic methods. The Sekem Academy located near Cairo undertakes applied research in agriculture and pharmaceuticals and helped to create the Heliopolis University which just recently opened and is offering degrees in pharmacy, engineering, and business. All students will take a set of core courses using a holistic approach to education focusing on culture, the environment, globalism, and the full development of personal abilities. In sum, Sekem in its short lifetime has created an impressive set of institutions with a visionary hope for realizing sustainable social and economic progress in the Egyptian countryside. How such a social invention occurred is a fascinating tale worthy of our attention.

Starting up something so unusual as an organic farm in an autocratic country dominated by the military and run by centralized bureaucracies proved to be a demanding and frustrating task. One day bulldozers and soldiers arrived on the Sekem farm and started pulling down three-year old trees to clear the land. A local general had decided to turn the farm into a military area to take advantage of a water supply from wells dug for crops, and the intrusion was brought to a halt only because Dr. Abouleish was friends with President Sadat and could ask for his help.

One of the biggest challenges to Sekem arose from pesticide spraying on neighboring cotton fields spilling over onto the farm's medicinal herbs and other organic crops, threatening the company's certification as a biodynamic producer. Fearing a collapse in the cotton crop, the Egyptian government refused to curtail pesticide spraying. Sekem set out to prove on test plots that organic methods to control pests can be just as functional and no more costly than conventional pesticide applications. After several years of testing, Sekem demonstrated the effectiveness of organic methods, and pesticide use was eventually halted on all of Egyptian cotton fields. As a reward for its efforts, Sekem successfully entered the organic cotton business.

Egyptian pesticide companies of course were unhappy about the loss of a lucrative market caused by Sekem and began a campaign to generate negative publicity against the company. Newspaper articles soon appeared suggesting that organic agriculture is unaffordable for poor countries like Egypt and that Sekem is a pawn of wealthy Europeans. The most damaging attack came with a widely circulated news report that the company's employees engaged in sun worship on the job, a practice seen as idolatrous and horrific to faithful Muslims. The news article grossly misrepresented a weekly employee assembly where all stand in a circle to emphasize the importance of each individual in the work of the whole and the equal dignity of everyone.

To combat attacks by prayer leaders in local mosques, Dr. Abouleish decided to invite all local Muslim community leaders, mayors, and sheiks to Sekem to show how the company's mission promotes important virtues of the Muslim faith. He used passages from the Koran to illustrate how organic agriculture meets the call for faithful Muslims to be "...responsible for the earth, plants and animals." To make his point more fully, Dr. Abouleish quoted the following from the Koran along with other similar passages:

> The sun and the moon pursue their ordered course. The plants and the trees bow down in adoration. He [God] raised the heaven on high and set the balance of all things, that you might not transgress it. Do not disrupt the equilibrium and keep the right measure and do not lose it.[101]

He went on in the meeting to explain exactly how biodynamic agricultural methods support the balance of nature more effectively than the kind of farming that makes heavy use of pesticides and fertilizers. The audience was impressed by the connection between organic agriculture and the call of the Koran for human stewardship of the Earth and nature. Positive articles about Sekem soon appeared in the Egyptian media and public doubts about the company evaporated.

This brief summary of Sekem's overcoming of early tribulations offers only a partial and incomplete picture of its accomplishments. For the complete story, I urge readers to take a look at Dr. Abouleish's inspiring book, *Sekem: A Sustainable Community in the Egyptian Desert.*

The Sekem experience demonstrates a potential in Egyptian agricultural for expansion and employment growth while at the same time doing good turns for both local rural communities and the environment. One of the biggest advantages Egypt and other north African countries such as Tunisia possess for organic food production is their proximity to European markets. Demand in Europe for organics has been growing rapidly in recent years, and the ability of Egypt to provide crops in all seasons is a special competitive benefit. Because of its reduced demand for water relative to conventional crops, organics place less pressure on scarce water resources, and since organics don't require pesticides or synthetic fertilizers, a transition to organic cropping in and adjacent to the Nile Valley would substantially diminish the region's water pollution problems. The buildup and retention of carbon in organically cropped soils and the reduced dependence on fossil fuel based pesticides and fertilizers that comes from a transition to organics has the positive side-benefit of diminishing the impact of agriculture on climate change. Since organic methods are often more labor intensive than mechanized conventional agriculture, a shift in cropping to organics would in itself increase employment. Perhaps the biggest benefit of Sekem's approach is its practice of creating farms on desert lands through the addition of compost to the soil and the development of highly efficient irrigation systems using deep wells. In this way, Egyptian agricultural production is expanded without placing added pressure on scarce Nile Valley land and water resources. Sekem can't be accused of ignoring the Egyptian need for good food since almost 70 percent of its total sales occur in the domestic market. The lucrative export market essentially provides added financial power to Sekem for investing in domestic agriculture to the benefit of Egypt as a whole. The point is simple: expansion of organic agriculture in Egypt and elsewhere can be good for both economic development and the environment, and in this endeavor Sekem offers an enticing model for solving a multitude of economic, social, and environmental problems in rural areas of the Middle East.

Ibrahim Abouleish is just one man who has successfully sought an intersection between the Muslim faith and European post-materialist values. In his life, he oriented himself both to the tenants of Islam, and to self-expression, individual freedom, tolerance for human differences, and environmental protection. Islamic scholars have little trouble constructing an environmental ethic rooted in the Koran and Islamic theology, but whether such ethical constructs matter in the political arena is the real question we have to address. The Sekem experience points to the potential for a sea change of environmental practice within the confines of Islamic teaching. The real issue is whether there is support for environmental improvement among those who possess real economic and political power. If the Arab Spring leads to full political democracy in Egypt, then the values of the public as a whole on this issue will be more likely to move to center stage and survey research suggests that the environment will be on the agenda. Philosophy again will matter, but it will now be a blending of Islam and post-materialism, and chances are social entrepreneurs such as Ibrahim Abouleish will be leading the charge to a better environmental and economic future.

***

To backyard gardeners who love to muck around in real dirt, growing plants in water somehow seems other-worldly   but the science of doing so, known as hydroponics, is a well established technology. Soil in natural conditions serves as a reservoir for water and plant nutrients, but plants don't actually require soil to survive. Nutrients are absorbed by plants through roots as inorganic mineral ions dissolved in water. So long as plant roots have access to water containing essential minerals, plants can survive without soil. Since plant survival also requires access to oxygen through roots, roots cannot be completely and perpetually immersed in water unless it is adequately aerated or else the plants will drown. Plants can be grown hydroponically in solution using something as simple as a water in a Mason jar, but more frequently growers use an inert medium in which to grow the plants such as perlite, gravel, mineral wool, or coconut husk.

Hydroponic gardening has virtues that offer special advantages for growing plants in an arid climate like Cairo's. In soil-based farming, applying the right amount of water is a tricky business. Too much watering causes plants to die from a lack of oxygen, and too little leads to plant starvation. For hydroponic farming, plant roots can be continuously or frequently exposed to nutrient-laden water and the plants can absorb as much or as little as they want. Unused water can be drained away and recycled keeping water use to a bare minimum. The key challenge for the hydroponic approach is to get the balance of needed mineral in the water just right, including macronutrients such as nitrates, calcium, phosphate, and magnesium, and micronutrients such as iron, copper, zinc, boron, chlorine and nickel. In addition to an appropriate balance of nutrients, care must be taken to not let the water's pH get out of whack or salts to build up excessively. Any interruption in water flows can be catastrophic, and water must be stored in light-free tanks to prevent the formation of algae. A successful hydroponic system can achieve high levels of productivity with a modest water and nutrient input.[102]

The other central ingredient in plant growth is sunshine, something that the rooftops of Cairo have in abundance year around. The city's low income residents have long used rooftops to raise chickens and goats but not to grow crops. Looking out over Cairo's rooftops from a minaret or any other high vantage points, one sees mostly accumulated debris, satellite dishes, and virtually nothing green. The dream of social entrepreneur, Sherif Hosny, is to create 325 hydroponic rooftop gardens in Cairo by 2013. Hosny named the business, Schaduf, after a simple traditional Egyptian tool for raising water to higher ground for crop irrigation. Sherif's brother, Tarek, will join the business after completing his college education in the U.S.

The business offers Cairo's poorest residents a simple form of hydroponic farming. Construct on a family's rooftop three 20 square meter ponds made of brick sides about 10 centimeters high and place a waterproof liner on the inner surface, fill with water and cover with sheets of floating styrofoam to serve as a platform for plants, and install a circulating pump for oxygenating the water. Add a standard hydroponic nutrient mix and plant the seedlings. Come by and check the pH and electrolyte levels weekly, replenish nutrients as needed, and soon with the help of Egypt's sun and heat you will have a rooftop of green produce that can be sold for 300-500 Egyptian pounds a month, significantly increasing a Cairene's family income and creating a wonderful place for children to play that pulls them away from the dangers of the streets. Sherif's company, Schaduf Urban Micro Farms, will provide a poor family with a rooftop farm costing about 4,000 Egyptian pounds that can be financed with a micro-loan easily paid off in a year. So far Schaduf has installed and maintains 15 farms, periodically checking the nutrient mix, controlling any pests organically, and collecting and selling the produce in a local Zamalek farmer's market for its clients.[103]

While visiting Cairo, my wife and I, along with our son and his boss, ate a celebratory dinner costing 2,000 Egyptian pounds at a fancy restaurant on the Nile called the Sequoia, a place where Cairenes go to be seen. This means roughly that a low-income rooftop garden costs about 8 Sequoia meal equivalents, an amount of money that doesn't mean much to us affluent westerners, but can make a huge difference to the lives of Cairo's urban farmers.

Leaving a successful career as the Middle East Regional Managing Director for mining Giant Rio Tinto Alcan, Sherif Hosny moved on to become a creator of rooftop gardens. Ask him why he gave up a lucrative career to take up urban farming, he will tell you that he wants to help others, likes working with plants, and desires to earn enough income to live on. In these motivations, Hosny differs little from Ibrahim Abouleish, the founder of Sekem. While he grew up in a Muslim family, Hosni doesn't claim that his faith played any special role in his decision to found Schaduf, yet what he is doing satisfies Islamic premises much like Sekem does.

Hosny chose to do a business rather a nongovernmental organization (NGO) so he wouldn't have to worry about raising money for operations, and he wanted the people he helps to have a vested interest themselves in sustaining the final product, the rooftop farm. If nothing else, Schaduf's clients will work hard to pay back the micro-loans they take out for their farms, and once they do, their take-home income jumps, encouraging them to keep their efforts up. NGOs are a part of the picture for rooftop farming and make a difference for Schaduf by helping to identify eligible clients and arranging micro-loans. The beauty of the whole venture is that it is self-funding and can be readily scaled up as the business grows.

Hosny continues to work on new ideas for rooftop farming, including an organic nutrient mix to replace the standard chemical variety. Schaduf's most important innovation to date has been the development of the simple brick-sided floor pond to replace the usual wooden racks hydroponic gardeners typically use for plant trays, which turn out to be uneconomical in Cairo because wood is too expensive. In the past Hosny experimented with an aquaponic approach to micro farming using tilapia, but the fish couldn't survive Cairo's winter temperatures in the shallow tanks required by a rooftop location, and heaters proved to costly for his low-income clients. Schaduf is considering selling rooftop hydroponic gardens to more affluent customers who want to grow their own plants and create a green space for their family. This would augment Schaduf's sales and income and increase the scale of its operation allowing the venture to better serve its low-income farmers.

Sherif Hosny fits the classic definition of a social entrepreneur, someone engaged in business to solve social or environmental problems, not just to earn profit. Schaduf and Hosny offer opportunities for poor families to increase their income, expand the supply of healthy greens for Cairenes, and create much needed green space in a city that has very little. In this effort, Hosny and Schaduf engage in social invention—the search for new and innovative methods for solving social and environmental problems. Schaduf not only applies a time-tested technology in a new way, but is creating a new form of pesticide-free agriculture that functions without fossil fuel inputs and requires very little water, a huge benefit in a desert environment. Schaduf, like any other entrepreneurial venture may or may not work out, and if it doesn't Hosny will move onto something else. Given the important functions Schaduf fulfills, I hope and suspect that it will succeed and contribute to a better future for Egyptians.

***

You may remember as a young child playing with a magnifying glass on a sunny day frying ants, burning holes in paper, or even starting a fire, much to you parents' horror. Concentrating solar power (CSP) works essentially the same way as your magnifying glass. In a CSP solar energy field, a series of parabolic mirrors capture and focus the suns energy, just like a magnifying glass, on special receiving pipes, heating up oil inside. The hot oil runs through a heat exchanger creating steam that in turn powers an electrical generator. The spent steam is condensed in a cooling tower and runs back to the heat exchangers to repeat the process. To keep the power plant running all night, part of the plant's solar capacity is used to store heat energy in molten salt for generating steam after the sun goes down. High voltage direct current lines are given the job of transmitting electricity to distant markets because their energy loss is only about 3 percent every 1,000 kilometers, much less than alternating current lines. Concentrating solar plants come in a variety of configurations including flat mirrors focused on a tower and mirrors arrayed in a dish focused on a central generating unit, but the most widely used technology is parabolic trough mirrors capable of tracking the sun.

CSP is the wave of the energy future for North Africa and the Middle East and by extension for deserts everywhere in the eyes of both the World Bank and DESERTEC, an international foundation devoted to the goal of producing clean energy from the world's deserts. A possible solar future is laid out for five countries, Morocco, Algeria, Tunisia, Egypt, and Jordan, in the World Bank's publication, "Middle East and North Africa Region Assessment of Local Manufacturing Potential for Concentrating Solar Power (CSP) Projects." This is a bureaucratic mouthful, but the study is must-reading for anyone who wants to learn about the potential of solar energy in hot desert landscapes.[104]

CSP is a tried, although not quite yet true, technology in terms of its cost competitiveness, with plants operating in the U.S., Spain, Morocco, Egypt, and elsewhere.

Currently, CSP can't match the low production costs of coal-fired power plants, but this will happen in the future as industry-wide scale economies and the technology learning curve that accompanies them are realized. CSP produces electricity currently at 0.14-0.18 Euros per kilowatt hour (KWh), but by the time 5 gigawatts (GW) of capacity is installed worldwide, this cost should fall to 0.08-0.12 Euros, which will be within shooting distance of the current average of 0.10 Euros per KWh for coal in Europe. Right now 2 GW of CSP capacity is either installed or under construction globally and another 12 GW is on the drawing boards. Utilities in Europe that burn coal today are required to purchase carbon emission allowances, which have been sell for around 10 Euros per metric ton.[105] This adds about 0.01 Euros to the cost per KWh which will rise after 2013 when emissions caps in Europe are tightened and the costs of allowances is projected to increase beyond 30 Euros per metric ton, boosting coal-fired costs to 0.13 Euros per KWh. At this point CSP will look better than coal as a long-term source for European electrical energy.

In North African, CSP will not only provide a secure and economical source of energy, but will also be a substantial employment generator for both the export and domestic energy markets. Under a scenario of aggressive growth in CSP capacity, the World Bank predicts that installed capacity will reach 5 GW by 2020 and will grow to 14.5 GW by 2025.

The recently completed construction of a hybrid CSP and natural gas plant at Kuraymat, Egypt, 90 miles south of Cairo, offers a preview of possible job opportunities. Of the 150 MW total capacity, the CSP portion will deliver 20-25 MW. Roughly 60 percent of the total project value for the solar portion flowed to local businesses who undertook site preparation and construction, provided the mounting structure, tubes, electrical cables, and carried out grid connections, engineering, and procurement. Local businesses and utility employees benefit permanently from carrying out the plant's operations and ongoing maintenance. The components unavailable locally and imported for Kuraymat included mirrors, the receiver, heat transfer fluid, and the steam generator. As the North African CSP market expands, some portion of these components can probably be produced locally, particularly mirrors and receivers. The Egyptian glass industry has grown both in capacity and sophistication in recent years and could become a future supplier of parabolic mirrors. Egyptian companies today not only manufacture the high-quality clear glass required for CSP mirrors, but are also able to bend glass into parabolic shapes and to coat it with a protective shield to defend against desert blowing sands. The suppliers of power generating equipment, such as General Electric and Siemens, have unmatchable specialized production experience that can't be duplicated locally, and such equipment will have to be imported as will molten salt heat storage facilities whose production is also highly specialized. Plant design will also be a global affair, but the supply of domestic engineering talent will expand as local educational institutions ramp up programs in solar technologies. A potentially important, but tough to document, spillover effect of a more technologically sophisticated local population will be innovation and employment creation in an array of related economic arenas. Knowledge begets new ideas, and new ideas beget new ways of making a living

For the North Africa-Middle East region, the World Bank forecasts the creation of 34,000 CSP-related permanent jobs by 2020 under its aggressive expansion alternative and 64,000-79,000 permanent jobs by 2025. These include both operation and maintenance employment and a permanent manufacturing and construction workforce to feed a continuous expansion of CSP for both the local and European market. This projection is based on achieving an installed capacity of 5 GW by 2020 and another 2 GW in equipment exports, and 14.5 GW installed by 2025 plus 5.2 GW of equipment exports. The job creation figures don't include multiplier effects that will lead to employment increases in the larger local economy. Newly hired workers will inject some portion of their new found income into the local economy as consumer spending which will in turn further expand employment and create still more income and spending. A multiplier effect of 1.5 times the initial CSP employment creation is not out of the question. Some North African countries, such as Egypt, possess significant oil and gas reserves, but the employment rate per unit energy is much less in fossil fuel than solar, and these reserves will ultimately be depleted while solar energy will be renewed daily as long as the sun shines. A solar future looks much better than continued reliance on fossil fuels.

Bringing solar power to the North African desert will be a huge undertaking requiring an unparalleled volume of social coordination and invention. The social entrepreneurship needed will exceed the capacity of any single business enterprise and will call for a coordinated effort that can be met only by governmental and nongovernment organizations. We don't normally think of not-for-profit enterprises, either within or outside of government, as being entrepreneurial, but reality needn't always accord with popular perception as we will now suggest.

The DESERTEC Foundation is one of those nongovernment organizations (NGOs) that just might make a difference in the world's energy future. Rather than retire and head for the golf course, Dr. Gerhard Knies, an expert in particle physics who spent his research career at such institutions as CERN and the University of California-Berkeley, founded in 2003 the Trans-Mediterranean Renewable Energy Cooperation, a network of experts in renewable energy. This organization in turn created the DESERTEC Foundation in 2009 to promote the development of solar energy in desert landscapes. The Foundation encourages academic research and training programs in renewable energy throughout Europe, North Africa, and the Middle East, pushes cooperative research programs with private businesses interested in renewable energy, and sets up programs with businesses to facilitate specific projects such as wind energy in Morocco and a 2 gigawatt concentrating solar plant in the Tunisian desert.[106]

Our energy future according to the thinkers at DESERTEC lies in the sun-drenched desert wastelands of the world. Hot deserts receive so much solar energy annually that no more than 1 percent of their 36 million square kilometers would be needed to replace present-day global fossil fuel energy consumption. Primary global energy consumption from fossil fuels currently equals 107,000 Terrawatt hours (TWh) a year, and a kilometer of hot desert receives 2.2 TWh of solar energy annually, of which 0.33 TWh can be captured at a presently attainable 15 percent electricity conversion rate. Even if total fossil fuel energy demand ultimately doubles, which exceeds current projections for the next half-century, no more than 2 percent of desert landscapes would be needed for solar energy production under the radical assumption that all of our fossil-fuel replacing energy comes from deserts.[107]

The experts at DESERTEC favor solar thermal technology, such as concentrating solar power (CSP) as opposed to photovoltaics, which generate electricity only when the sun shines. As we already know, solar thermal plants can collect heat energy in the daytime and store it for use at night, allowing around-the-clock electrical energy production. A drawback of solar thermal technology is its potential to disturb the ecology of certain sensitive desert landscapes. Some deserts, such as the Sonoran and Mohave in the U.S., contain threatened species, but avoiding the destruction of rare habitat seems reasonable under a solar energy regime through careful placement of solar thermal facilities given the huge amount amount of desert landscape available worldwide.[108] In sensitive habitats, photovoltaic panels may be the better technology to use because they needn't be installed in the more disturbing large scale facilities typical of solar thermal. Solar panels can be tucked in along exists roads and power lines without doing much damage. At some point in the future, using daytime solar energy to produce hydrogen through electrolysis will become cost effective which can then be stored and used for 24-hour electricity generation. Hydrogen powered fuel cells that produce electric energy have a variety of potential applications including running motor vehicles or supplying electricity on demand.

In the near term, a clean energy future for Europe and the Mediterranean Basin includes a substantial role for concentrating solar-based energy production (CSP) from the deserts of North Africa. DESERTEC envisons an installed CSP capacity in North Africa by 2050 of 400 GW with 100 of that serving the European energy market. Using the World Bank's projection of 25 one-year local jobs per MW of installed capacity, this means that an average of 250,000 manufacturing and construction jobs per year would need between 2011 and 2050 to reach 400 GW of installed capacity. To permanently maintain 400 GW of capacity after 2050, including end-of-life equipment replacement, will require approximately 320,000 permanent jobs, based on studies of existing thermal solar plants. With a continuous growth of CSP in North Africa of 4 GW annually, CSP employment will reach 570,000 by 2050, and continue to grow slowly after that. This will be a substantial addition of jobs for the North African labor force, which is currently about 60 million for the CSP-coalition countries.

Big solar energy projects in the North African desert have gone beyond the abstract discussion phase and are now coming into reality. One of the most ambitious of these is the proposed TuNur CSP plant to be located in the southern Tunisian desert. TuNur, a DESERTEC supported project, will deliver 2,000 megawatts of energy into the Italian electrical grid through a direct current high energy line under the Mediterranean beginning in 2016. TuNur is a joint venture between British solar developer, Nur Energie, and a Tunisian company, Top Oilfield Services, and will use a system of large mirrors to concentrate the sun's energy on solar towers to heat molten salt that in turn generates steam to run electric generators continuously day and night. By recycling the steam, water inputs to the system will be minimal and the impact on the desert landscape modest. Project investment and operations will create 20,000 local jobs in mirror fabrication, plant construction, and maintenance. On completion, TuNur will be the largest solar energy project in the world. Top Oilfield Services' bread and butter in the past has been servicing the petroleum industry, but ironically its future looks to be in desert-based solar where its desert experience will be a special advantage. If TuNur succeeds, it will train a generation of Tunisian engineers and technicians in solar energy and set the foundation for a new source of employment in the country's future.[109]

To think about clean and green economic development on such a huge scale as DESERTEC's vision for a solar future can be mind boggling. In reality, creating a compact green economy in North Africa and elsewhere will involve an accumulation of many different approaches and technologies and the work of all sorts of entrepreneurs, social and otherwise, at a range of scales.[110] To illustrate opportunities in a wider arena, let's consider two on the ground concrete examples that function on a smaller in scale than CSP but could ultimately have a substantial economic and environmental impact.

**

Ahmed Zahran grew up in Cairo, received a bachelor's degree in finance from the American University in Cairo, and a masters from the University of London. While he never was exposed to renewable energy in his studies, he gained an interest in it early on, and wanted to work in the field. Because opportunities were nonexistent in Egypt, Zahran went work for Shell Oil Company and eventually landed in the company's carbon emissions trading department. Here it soon became obvious to him that the only way to reduce emissions was to shift from fossil fuels to solar, and his work at Shell was not going to help much in achieving that goal.[111]

Zahran returned to Egypt and went to work for a solar energy company that unfortunately succumbed to the upheaval of the Arab Spring. This experience led Zahran to join with some friends in founding KarmSolar for the purpose of developing solar energy applications to serve the unique needs of Egyptians who live in desert landscapes. KarmSolar has gained global attention for its work on high capacity off-grid solar water pumps that recover underground water from very deep wells for agricultural uses. The essential premise of KarmSolar is to offer Egyptians the opportunity to live in off-grid desert communities and have access to essential unexploited groundwater resources available on the edges of the Nile Valley and desert oases. The idea is to pull population away from an overcrowded Nile and take advantage of the desert's abundance of sun and soil.

The standard approach for Nile Valley irrigation agriculture is to simply flood the fields periodically to supply water to plants. In reclaimed desert reliant on scarce groundwater, flooding is too wasteful. Movable sprinklers and drip irrigation systems offer a much more water efficient approach to growing crops. Sprinkler irrigation turns out not to be very effective for anything but low value fodder crops because of leaf salt-burn on broadleaf plants or problems with fungi forming because of water accumulation on leaf surfaces. Drip irrigation systems, with perforated plastic piping laid out in rows adjacent to vegetable or fruit plants, offer a highly efficient method of water and liquid fertilizer delivery to plant roots. In this sense, drip irrigation and hydroponic agriculture bear a similarity. Some drip irrigation farmers take advantage of a lucrative nearby European organic fruit and vegetable market by creating liquid organic fertilizer from animal manure onsite for delivery to plants through the irrigation system. One might think that the investment requirement rules out out all but big farms for drip irrigation, but already in desert landscapes hired workers learn the drip irrigation ropes and install inexpensive drip systems on their own nearby small plots.[112]

The big problem currently for agriculture on reclaimed Egyptian desert far away from an electrical grid is dependence on diesel powered generators that require difficult to deliver and expensive liquid fuels for their operation. The big advantage offered by the KarmSolar approach is an independent local source of electrical power that can run irrigation pumps and other kinds of equipment such as water purifiers and desalinators. The marriage of solar power and water efficient-irrigation makes feasible the creation of new communities in the desert wherever groundwater can be found. Not only does this opportunity allow KarmSolar to make money to sustain itself, but also opens up a chance for Egyptians to find a new ways of making a living without having to depend on an unreliable electrical grid or an incompetent central government. This is to the liking of social entrepreneurs such as KarmSolar's Ahmed Zahran and Schaduf's Sherif Hosny who express concerns about government incompetence. It's fascinating to see entrepreneurial efforts with both a social and an environmental mission, such as Sekem, Schaduf, and KarmSolar, gaining a foothold in the context of government ineffectiveness, political upheaval, and a strongly traditional Muslim culture. This is not say that government always lacks the capacity for social invention as we will now demonstrate with an example from another country suffering through tumultuous political times, Tunisia.

***

Back in the days of the first energy crisis (early 1980s), installing rooftop solar panels was all the rage, only it wasn't for generating electricity. To do that, one would need photovoltaics, but those were prohibitively expensive at the time. Rather, individuals on the cutting edge of energy conservation were installing rooftop solar panels for the purpose of heating water. The insulated glass-covered panels consisted of small pipes set in heat-absorbing fins through which liquid circulated for exposure to the sun's rays. With the subsequent crash in energy prices, rooftop water heaters went out of fashion, but the technology didn't disappear. Today rooftop water heaters are back in a part of the world where they truly make sense, the Middle East. In Palestine, 76 percent of households have installed solar water heaters as a countermeasure to the Israeli ability to cut off electricity at any moment. Even if the lights go out, Palestinians still have hot water.[113]

With help from the United Nations Environmental Program (UNEP) and the Italian-led Mediterranean Renewable Energy Program (MEDREP), the Tunisian Government instituted a program in 2005 called Prosol (Program Solaire) to encourage the installation of rooftop water heaters. To get one, a homeowner goes to a solar water heater supplier, fills out an application, presents a utility bill, signs a loan agreement with a bank for a 5-year repayment from the monthly energy cost savings, and makes a 10 percent down payment. Loan payments are added to customer gas and electric bills, and if payments fall in arrears, the utility has the option of shutting off service. In the first two years of the program, interest costs were subsidized partly by banks because of a low risk of nonpayment and partly by the UNEP, and MEDREP funded a 20 percent capital cost subsidy for the heaters. After 2006, the Tunisian government took over funding of the capital subsidy and exempted solar heaters from the VAT tax and a portion of the customs duty on imported units. As of 2010, approximately 356,000 square meters of heater panels have been installed in 119,000 households and the annual installation rate had risen to 80,000 square meters. As a direct result of the program, 1,100 qualified installers found employment, 3,500 total jobs have been created in 50 companies, and households will save a total of $600-1,300 (U.S.) on their energy bills over the solar heater's lifetime. Conversions to solar heating in Tunisia to date has reduced annual CO_2 emissions by 755,000 tons, a number that will rise to 1.95 million tons by 2016 given a projected total of 376,000 installations.[114]

We normally think of governments as slow-to-change bureaucracies wedded to rule-oriented procedures in the delivery of government services. The Prosol case offers us an interesting example of entrepreneurial social invention by a government. While governments don't always rise to the need for new ideas in addressing social and environmental problems, in some instances they do, just like socially inventive businesses or nongovernmental organizations such as a Sekem or a DESERTEC. Just as many other governments in Middle Eastern and Africa, Tunisia subsidizes household energy costs for the alleged purpose of alleviating poverty. Economists have long attacked such subsidies for causing wasteful energy consumption, excessive air pollution, and added greenhouse gas emissions, and failing to benefit the poor very much. Unfortunately, energy subsidies of this kind are politically challenging to eliminate because doing so raises energy costs for a large portion of the population. By supporting and subsidizing the installation of fossil fuel replacing solar water heaters, the Tunisian government reduced the need to pay out subsidies for fossil fuel energy to the tune of $100 million, a figure that will fall to $46 million if a proposed subsidy phase-out plan is actually implemented, but enough to still more than cover the $22 million government outlay for the Prosol program. In short, Prosol provides a special financial benefit to the Tunisian government which undoubtedly helped motivate the program in the first place. Another financial boost equalling $350,000-700,000 annually comes to Tunisia from sales of Prosol generated greenhouse emissions reduction certificates (CERs) to European countries under the Kyoto Clean Development Mechanism. Once a projected 376,000 solar heating units are installed by 2016, the annual revenue flow from CERs should triple. If any single agency got the ball rolling for Prosol, it would have to be the UNEP who did the original study setting out all the program's possible benefits.

The simple idea of solar water heating has brought the Tunisian people reduced utility bills, more business activity and employment, reduced government costs, increased revenues from Europe for CERs, and reduced dependency on fossil fuels. Because of Prosol, the planet as a whole benefits from lower` greenhouse gas emissions. Compact clean energy in this instance amounts to economic boon and a true free lunch for Tunisia. Other countries including

Egypt have seen the Prosol light emanating from Tunisia and are now starting their own programs.

***

The outward growth of cities, and the move to a more spatially expansive mode of living, has now become global in extent. The decline in urban density and the move to an auto-dominated system of urban transit has been most extreme in the U.S. compared to the rest of the world. Urban density in Europe is almost four times as great as the U.S. and in the Middle East nearly eight times as great. The affluent cities of western Europe are much more compact than comparable American cities, and the low income cities of the Middle East such as Cairo are among the most compact in the world. If the growing and developing cities of the Middle East, Africa, Latin America, and Asia adopt an American-style love affair with the motor vehicle and dramatically reduce their urban densities as a consequence, global urban carbon emissions will skyrocket. If these cities instead follow a European model and stick with high density living, the results will be much less damaging to the climate. Judging from the volume of motor vehicle traffic in Cairo and Istanbul, Middle Eastern cities may be edging toward the American model just at the point when Americans are re-considering the virtues of low density living and choosing to reside in more compact central cities. Is it possible for the developing cities of the world to short-circuit the suburbanization process the West and stick with high-density living? Will social inventions and innovations that promote continued high density living be adopted by low-income cities experiencing economic improvement? Let's investigate this possibility for Cairo, Egypt.

Cairo is among the largest, densest, and oldest cities in the world. The city today is at the pinnacle of global compact urban living with the average Cairene managing on less than one seventh of urban land as an average Chicagoan. Most residents of urban Cairo live in some of the densest neighborhoods in the world, giving them less than a fourth of the land area per person enjoyed by the average Parisian who lives much more compactly than most Europeans. Cairo extends in a narrow corridor along the Nile River with desert looming to both the east at west at the dividing point between upper and lower Egypt. To the north of the city, the Nile's floodplain begins to fan out as multiple channels form and find their way to the Mediterranean. Without the Nile and its agriculturally rich floodplain, Egypt as we know it today with its great historical treasures would not exist. Of Egypt's 73 million inhabitants, 95 percent crowd into 4 percent of the country's land area that makes up the Nile Valley and Delta. With the exception of a few oases and coastal areas, the remainder of the country is uninhabited, hot desert. Since the 1930s, the population of greater Cairo has increased from a million to more than seventeen million residents. Through 1980, the growth of Cairo could be explained mainly by rural to urban migration within Egypt, but since then population growth in metro Cairo driven by high birth rates has become predominantly an internal affair.[115]

A first-time traveller to Cairo can easily be overwhelmed by an array of intense visual and aural stimuli: beautiful mosques, unrelenting traffic, the haunting call to prayer, urban noise, hundreds of unfinished but occupied concrete and masonry multi-storied buildings, the beautiful Nile, crowded sidewalks and markets, pedestrians dodging through traffic, garbage, mysterious women in colorful head scarves, men in traditional dress, kids everywhere, police on every corner with weapons at the ready, the pyramids off in the distance, and covering it all a blanket of air pollution. Our new traveller will soon discover that getting from one point to another in the city poses a serious challenge. Sitting in traffic is an inevitable daily pastime, burning up a half a billion dollars in fuel yearly. The fastest way of getting around is Cairo's metro, but it provides access to less than a third of the city and accounts for only a bit more than a sixth of individual trips within the city. Half of all trips are taken in private minibuses, shared taxies, and overcrowded municipal buses. Despite an explosion in automobile traffic, most Cairenes can't afford private cars. Only about 10 percent of Cairo families possess motor vehicles and those account for just 20 percent of urban travel. Taxies are everywhere and supply 29 percent of all trips, but private cars lead the way in Cairo's traffic congestion because of their numbers and low occupancy rates.[116]

By global standards, Egyptians consume very little energy per person and emit little carbon, but as the country advances economically, both are on the rise. Of 84 global cities, Cairo is fifth up from the bottom of the list for per capita transport-related carbon emission (Atlanta, Georgia is at the top).[117] Notwithstanding the auto-induced air pollution one sees in Cairo, the city still attains high energy efficiency per person and correspondingly low carbon emissions because of both its high density and poverty, much like many other low-income cities worldwide.[118] An emerging love affair with the automobile among Cairo's elite nonetheless bodes ill for the future. If individual Egyptian incomes continue to advance at their recent pace, then more and more Cairenes will be able to afford cars, and, without new mass transit alternatives, the city's traffic will become increasingly frozen and air pollution more intense.

Cairo's compactness today has little to do with urban planning and much to do with how low income housing has been created in the past forty years. For most of Cairo residents, housing supplied legally in the formal housing market is simply unaffordable. The gap in housing supply for almost two-thirds of metropolitan Cairo residents has been filled by an informal market functioning outside of land use law and building codes.[119]

Because cropland along the Nile is privately owned and desert lands to the east and west are in government hands, private lands are favored for housing construction at Cairo's edge for their more secure ownership tenure. The government can kick squatters off desert lands, but it can't easily evict owners from legally titled private lands. The military and various government agencies control desert parcels convenient to Cairo but are not about to relinquish them for informal housing, pushing development onto privately owned agricultural lands. For government to bring informal housing construction to a halt by draconian means would cause a huge housing supply crisis no one wants. Because informal housing construction is focused mostly on privately owned agricultural parcels, Egypt looses upwards of 400 hectares of prime cropland a year due to Cairo's expansion, a loss that many say the country can ill-afford given that only about 4 percent of its total land area is arable. In reality the 2,300 hectares lost to development on agricultural lands has been more than offset by the thousands of hectares added annually to cultivation by desert reclamation projects elsewhere in Egypt. To economize on scarce and expensive urban land, informal housing is constructed at very high densities matching those in any of Cairo's historic, Medieval-era districts, an outcome confirmed in aerial photo comparisons of the two kinds of neighborhoods.

The informal housing development process begins with a farmer subdividing and selling land to individuals or families who wish to construct dwellings. New landowners then put up dwellings for their own use or to generate income from rentals or sale. Frequently, an owner will construct a one or two story concrete and masonry building to start, move in, and add on three or four stories more as soon as money can be saved up. Because of this staged pattern of construction, communities on Cairo's edge have a perpetually unfinished look about them. Much of the informal housing in existence today was originally paid for with remittances from Egyptians working abroad in the oil-rich Gulf states. For builders to follow the letter of the law for subdivisions and building codes would be much too costly, and the government is not about to follow the drastic step of tearing down existing, much needed housing just because it doesn't happen to comply with current regulations.

The norm in third-world large-city informal housing is rickety shanty-towns, but Cairo is very much the exception.

Families, who put up most of Cairo's informal housing, act as their own contractors and carefully control quality in constructing simple, but solidly built concrete and masonry structures. A typical building will occupy a footprint of about 100 square meters and rise up to as high as five stories, with one or two apartments per floor. Again, construction usually occurs in stages, with one or two floors to start. Rooms are arranged around a central stair well and air shaft, and include a kitchen, living area, and one or two bedrooms. The provision of potable water, electricity, and sewerage hookups for informal housing is slow to arrive, and often requires substantial payments and bribes to government officials by building owners, but the more than 90 percent of housing in Cairo's informal areas have all three services. This is not to say that their functioning is very reliable. Plugged sewers, broken water mains, and electricity blackouts occur with some frequency in most areas. Lanes between buildings are narrow with little sunlight penetrating to street level, and public open space is absent. The main access roads in informal areas get created by filling in old irrigation canals, and many of the lanes are old irrigation laterals. While informal neighborhoods suffer from poor air circulation, traffic congestion, and a lack of public facilities such as schools and clinics, they are more than just warehouses for the poor and breeding grounds for crime and revolution. They possess extensive kinship networks, a vibrant street life, active mosques, local markets, employment in stores and small shops, connections to larger Cairo through ubiquitous private minibuses, and a core of middle class families.

The single biggest government effort to provide housing has been the planned creation of eight, spatially expansive, satellite suburban new towns in the desert outside of the built-up Cairo urban area. In laying out these new towns, government planners adopted a western suburban vision of spread out, auto oriented residential subdivisions, shopping malls, and industrial and office parks with the hope of diverting population expansion away from the city, but, contrary to the portrayal of a dream-like suburbia in the many billboards and ads one encounters in and around Cairo, the new towns have been an unmitigated failure. Simply put, new town housing is inaccessible or unaffordable for all but a small minority of Cairo's residents. To get into Cairo from new towns via minibuses for work takes way too long even if housing were cheap enough. To make the commute with ease requires owning a car, something that, as we already noted, very few Cairenes can afford. Despite a huge public investment in roads, sewers, water, street lightning, public spaces, landscaping, and treatment plants, the new towns count for only about 10 percent (1.8 million) of greater Cairo's population today on some 1,200 square kilometers. This amount of land is equivalent to about 70 percent of Cairo's current built-up urban area which houses nearly 15 million people. Vast plots of new town subdivided land remains undeveloped, and numerous new housing units remain unoccupied. The suburban dream so far in Cairo has turned out to be a dismal flop.

The future of housing in Cairo looks to be not in new towns, but in existing, compact, energy efficient, informal neighborhoods, and, given their past success in supplying reasonably decent housing at an affordable cost, this is a good thing. Cairo's housing future will brighten further if a more democratic and responsive government eventually brings an improvement in basic local services, especially garbage collection, and in transportation, education, and public open space. In the meantime, more inexpensive rooftop gardens would be a plus for bringing green space and nutritious food to Cairo's informal neighborhoods, a serious opportunity for Schaduf's rooftop farms and micro-financing NGOs.

Despite its current poverty and political troubles, Egypt's material and social development improved markedly in the past few decades. The UN's Human Development Index, which is based on per capita Gross Domestic Product (GDP), life expectancy at birth, infant mortality, and schooling, increased in recent reports for

Egypt at an annualized rate of 1.5 percent a year, nearly matching the booming Asia/Pacific region.[120] The index goes beyond pure economic growth and accounts for both health and educational attainment. Improvements in the country's human development suggests that Egypt's Arab Spring may well have flowed less from material depravation than a growing desire for political freedom and democracy. Social science research on global human development processes tell us this: improved material and physical security along with increased educational attainment bring forth demands for more extensive self-expression, both personal and political.[121] Once attained, self-expression in its turn fosters more effective democratic governance and increases political demands for a variety of social goals, including gender equity, economic justice, racial tolerance, and environmental protection.

The emergence of democracy in Egypt will likely be a messy and protracted affair, but once it gains a foothold we can expect a growing public interest in government actions favorable to compact living and the environment. Less developed countries such as Egypt express greater concern for economic security and less for personal autonomy and individual freedom than the affluent west, but younger generations of Egyptians, who have grown up in a world with less infant mortality, improved health, and greater educational attainment, express post-material values with greater frequency than their older peers according to recent research based on the World Values Survey. Yet Egyptians as a whole continue a powerful commitment to traditional religious values and don't yet score very highly on aggregate measures of self-expressive values.[122] While tensions run high between Egyptian youth and their more traditional elders around such questions as personal freedoms and gender equity, the two groups seem to be in agreement on protection of the environment, especially in Cairo where environmental degradation is a part of the daily experience. Historically, environmental action has been suppressed by a dictatorial government whose predominant interest is in political control. Unleashing the forces of democracy will no doubt take Egypt in unexpected directions, but a path to environmental improvement that helps retain urban compactness is a distinct possibility. Simple social inventions are available to Cairenes that can bring substantial environmental improvement, support a continued compact form of urban life, and expand much needed employment opportunities. Let's consider a few of the more important examples.

Cairo already operates two modern underground metro rail lines, but they only serve about thirty percent of the city. If all lines currently on the drawing boards for Cairo were constructed, metro access would be expanded to most of the city's neighborhoods. A shift from commuting by minibus, taxi, and private automobile to riding the metro would bring substantial reductions in traffic congestion and local air pollution as well as climate-warming carbon emissions. The ease of getting around Cairo would be vastly improved, making it a more convenient and pleasant city to live in. A key economic virtue of metro rail expansion would be the huge number of construction jobs created, not only for the rail line themselves, but for the commercial and residential construction that will follow near metro stations. An efficient metro could be complimented with investment in a feeder system of dedicated bus lanes and low-emission hybrid buses.[123]

Expanding the metro underground rail system is neither an especially innovative nor new idea. The real need for social invention here is in the financing of such a project given that Egypt remains a relatively poor country with limited resources for such a huge investment. Nonetheless, Egyptians could take advantage of a funding source already in hand. The Egyptian government currently spends a fifth of its budget on energy subsidies, primarily for gasoline, amounting to roughly 6 percent of the country's GDP, or 30 billion dollars (U.S.) a year.[124] By any standard, this is a huge amount of money and constitutes a substantial source of funding. Such subsidies could be slowly reduced over time with the bulk of the reductions coming after transit projects are up and running and can provide inexpensive alternatives for Cairenes to get around. The up front costs of such projects could be borrowed from such global sources as the World Bank against future government revenues realized from reduced fuel subsidies. The Tunisian experience at a smaller scale with its Prosol solar water heater project sets a precedent for this approach in funding carbon pollution reduction projects.

Other "low-hanging" projects that yield significant greenhouse house gas and air pollution reductions are already in the works and would benefit from a financing boost. Conversion of taxis and minibuses to compressed natural gas as fuel is currently being promoted and could be moved along with incentives for vehicle conversion and refueling station construction.[125] Even with an improved underground metro system, minibuses and taxis will continue to be an essential piece of Cairo's transportation pie. A second step bringing further emissions reductions would be the introduction of a system of electric powered taxis and minibuses. Deals could be struck with automakers for job-expanding final assembling of such vehicles in Egypt, and a leasing system established to avoid the need for individual operators to bear the initial purchase cost. A side benefit of electric vehicles would be a substantial reduction in traffic noise. Of course, added clean sources of electric power will be needed for both the metro and electric vehicles. Egypt possesses a substantial potential for wind energy in the Gulf of Suez and projects to develop it are in the planning stage, and, as we know, the Egyptian desert offers some of the highest solar potential in the world. Good solar sites already being developed along the edge of the Nile Valley not far from existing power lines. Again, the key need for all this is creative financing spearheaded by an entrepreneurial Egyptian government. Given its history, such creativity seems unlikely, but with democracy and realization of obvious opportunities for much needed economic expansion, who knows. A free, energized, smart Egyptian population demanding a more responsive government is already being unleashed by the Arab Spring, but patience will be required by those pressing for a different and better future. The democracy learning curve can be lengthy, and powerful political forces wedded to the past will have to be overcome.

***

Cairo taxi drivers often ask whether my wife and I are Christians, a question for which I have yet to come up with a brief but satisfactory answer. In Egypt you are either Muslim or Christian, but nothing else it seems. Egyptians for the most part don't seem to understand what it means to be an agnostic, atheist, humanist, or universalist. Sometimes I say I am a pantheist, but I usually get a puzzled look, and we move onto talk about other things, such as how bad the traffic is in Cairo. Egyptians who are not Coptic usually say they are Muslim, although some don't seem very serious about their faith much like many Christian Americans, and many Egyptians we encounter frequently advocate for unhindered self-expression and personal freedoms. Those that do are strong supporters of the Arab Spring and creation of democracy in Egypt. Egyptian commitment to entrepreneurialism in the informal economy is palpable and can be seen everywhere on the streets with any good or service imaginable being offered for sale to passers-by. The extent of social entrepreneurialism in the country is less apparent, but, as our examples in this post show us, enterprises with a social mission can gain a foothold in Egypt (and Tunisia) despite hindrances from oppressive, authoritarian government bureaucracies.

The real danger confronting both Egyptian and Tunisian democracy comes from religious fundamentalists who want to quash expanding desires for fully free self-expression and gender equity. Doing so could divert political energies away from social improvement and dampen the entrepreneurial spirit essential to economic and environment progress. Yet there is a common path to a greener and more prosperous future in Egypt and

Tunisia that can be followed together by thoughtful post-materialists and Muslims. These two groups may part company on their interpretations of life's ultimate meaning and final cause, but they can agree on the importance of environmental improvement, climate stability, democracy, economic progress and equity, and individual freedom.

Chapter 13: What Philosophy for a Green Economic Future? Summing Up

The most important philosophical questions we all face are simple in their statement: Why do we exist at all? How should we lead our lives? What purposes should we pursue? What is the meaning of our being? One place to look for answers is in an organized religion that accepts on faith the idea of a final godly force in the universe that determines all else. The intellectually inclined can turn instead to a metaphysical philosophy that looks to final ideas as explainers of the universe and sources of meaning. Or one can set aside issues of finality as ultimately unprovable, or as lacking in interest for the pragmatics of daily life, and look to construct our purposes out of the raw material of the world as we find it. Whatever path to meaning we take, we have to adopt or create principles to live by, hopefully with mutual tolerance for each other's choices.

The pursuit of purpose and meaning in the world today takes an increasingly post-materialist form among younger, economically secure individuals who place their highest priority on free self-expression, a quality material environment, acquiring experiences, and advancing tolerance, justice, and protection of the earth. This doesn't mean that post-materialists are totally lacking in self-concern. When push comes to shove, we all protect our own first, but when our own position in the world is secure, we have the capacity to expand the content of our worldly concerns beyond an immediate circle of special interest. The rise of post-materialism means simply that once we achieve minimal benchmarks of material security, we shift some of our energy to broader concerns. Economists often argue that we will always find more private material wants to engage us, but research on post-materialism documents an expanding horizon of human interest beyond a strict materialist self-orientation to include, among other things, a public desire to bring climatic warming under control and to leave more disturbance-free space for nature.

In this final chapter, I want to take time to consider more concretely the essential features of a kind of philosophy I see taking hold over the long haul that will have a salutary impact earth's natural and human environment. Philosophers usually stick to the world of ideas without much attention to the messy details of worldly reality, ideas that are wonderful in and of themselves, but that need to be confronted with the actualities of natural and human history, something I have tried to do in these pages. For cynics my conclusions might be unbearably optimistic, but my only point in the end will be to claim that there is reason for hope. History is messy and depressing, but this doesn't rule out the possibility of a better future.

Belief in God and participation in organized religion is on the wane worldwide, although the U.S. stands fairly high in active church membership at 38 percent of the population as opposed to less than 10 percent for many European countries. In line with post-materialist trends, U.S. religious attendance by those in younger birth cohorts is declining significantly, and as these individuals age their attendance doesn't go up by much. This doesn't bode well for the future of organized religion, even in the U.S. where membership is comparatively high by global standards. Of course religion globally still matters in many parts of the developing world, as a quick perusal of the news on any given day will attest. The take away point here is that there is an inexorable trend away from religious commitment in affluent countries driven mainly by generational replacement, a phenomenon that necessarily works itself out slowly over time.[126]

If a rising portion of the global population is shifting away from conventional religion, what does this mean for the protection of our earthly environment? Will the decline of beliefs oriented to a heavenly afterlife bring us back to focusing on the world we live in, or will the loss of a commitment to a stewardship of God's creation lead to indifference about the fate of the earth? These are speculative questions, but worth pondering if one cares about the future of nature's wonders. I have no intention of extensively parsing the effects of organized religion on environmental concern and will leave that to others. What I want to do here instead is set out the features of a post-materialist, unaffiliated spirituality and what it could mean for environmental concern. First, I want to go back to what might seem like unlikely sources for ideas on what a secular spirituality might look like, Friedrich Nietzsche and Martin Heidegger. To put the question more bluntly, will the death of the god of organized religion kill off environmentalism, or cause it to flourish? A little attention to textual detail for these two thinkers I think will pay us a special dividend of a deeper understanding of what it is to be spiritual but not formally religious. Bear with me and see what we get.

***

The oddest but in many ways the most interesting of Nietzsche's writings is *Thus Spake Zarathustra*, a novel of sorts that is at once philosophical, polemical, and allegorical. It is the one work that stands as a comprehensive summary of Nietzsche's basic views. My intension here is to bring out what I would call Nietzsche's secular spirituality by interpreting key passages that refer specifically to the "earth."

Nietzsche is the ultimate anti-metaphysical philosopher. To ponder a final, god-like cause for all of existence is a waste of time. The world is what it is and look to it for your own meanings. Be a self-creator. Today Nietzsche would probably be an anarchistic libertarian who would hold little truck with the power of big institutions to run the show, and he would love the trend away from a mindless materialism and toward a free, self-expressive form of life. This we have already talked about in earlier chapters and don't need to rehash here. What I do want to look at more thoroughly is Nietzsche's attitude towards the Earth and nature as expressed in *Thus Spoke Zarathustra*.

Get over your slavish attachment to an otherworldly and heavenly beings. Come down to Earth and get beyond your sins. Create your being here on Earth and avoid sinning against it in the process. This constitutes what a humanity with new values will do in Nietzsche's eyes:

> Once the sin against God was the greatest sin, but God died, and these sinners died with him. To sin against the Earth is now the most dreadful thing. [127]

Forgetting about heavenly concerns is old stuff for Nietzsche, but worrying about the fate of the Earth now gets new and special attention. One could the see Earth as important only for satisfying urges of the new self-creator, the overman, Nietzsche's metaphor for what humanity ought to be:

> I love those who do not first seek behind the stars for a reason to go under and be a sacrifice, but who sacrifice themselves for the earth, that the Earth may some day become the overman's. [128]

We must first sacrifice for the earth, but eventually it will become ours for our use. But this interpretation fails to match up with a clearly reverent tone toward earthly being:

> It is an earthly virtue that I love; there is little prudence in it, and least of all the reason of all men. But this little bird built its nest with me: therefore I love and caress it; now it dwells with me, siting on its golden eggs...Let your gift-giving love and your knowledge serve the meaning of the earth... Do not let them fly away from earthly things and beat their wings against eternal walls. Alas, there has always been so much virtue that has flown away. Lead back to Earth the virtue that flew away, as I do—back to the body, back to life, that it may give the Earth a meaning, a human meaning. [129]

Nietzsche offers in *Thus Spoke Zarathustra* a new kind of secular spirituality. Spirit is in our home, the earth, as opposed to an otherworldly, heavenly place beyond our perceptive capacities. As a part of a new scheme of valuations, we as thinking beings look more to reflecting realistically about the content of our world, not of some imagined ideal place. We don't seek power over the Earth for exploitative ends, but to create on the Earth symbols of the sacredness of all beings:

> You still want to create the world before which you can kneel: that is your ultimate hope and intoxication...This I should like best...to love the Earth as the moon loves her, and to touch her beauty only with my eyes.[130]

We exercise power, but in the pursuit of creative ends, not for its own sake, and in the process we treat the Earth and its contents with respect and reverence. Our metaphysics is not abstract or ethereal, but oriented to the realities within which we live. Throughout *Thus Spoke Zarathustra*, the Earth and nature come off with a sense of amazement and wonder, not as simple objects to be exploited for material ends. Spirituality is pantheistic, a part of daily life. Life tragically has its sufferings and ends in death, but their is solace in returning to the earth:

> Thus want to die myself that you, my friends, may love the Earth for my sake; and to Earth I want to return that I may find rest in her who gave birth to me.[131]

This is the ultimate eternal return of the same, and it's earthly, not otherworldly.

What I take from Nietzsche here is the idea that one doesn't have to subscribe to final cause-based religions to be counted as spiritual. Nor does one need to have a metaphysical belief that primal ideas are waiting to be discovered that offer an explanation of why beings exist rather than not. A pragmatic spirituality is an option that sets aside such questions and focuses instead on the wonders of daily life.

***

Heidegger's thinking about how humans authentically relate to earthly existence bears a similarity to Nietzsche's. We get into trouble solidifying and finalizing our basic metaphysical assumptions about Being as a whole, such as the treatment of the universe as a collection of objects whose mechanisms of existence and functioning are ultimately discoverable. We get stuck at what we think is a well-defined horizon of Being, and fail to look beyond it.

For Heidegger a better understanding of beings and their interconnections takes us beyond science to poetry, which is more capable of expressing a mystery of existence that can never be discovered with finality. Instead of banking on an ultimate explanation, we best approach the meaning of Being with fascination and a constant questioning. In short, we can never arrive at Being's final horizon but we can push our horizon of understanding forward. We can continuously discover new interpretations and pragmatic principles, scientific and otherwise, that help us through daily life, but mysteries will always remain, giving us cause to look to nature with humility, respect, and a perpetual sense of wonder.

Heidegger's most direct discussion of the relationship between nature and humanity occurs in "What Are Poets For," a work where he sees poets as replacing shamans and priests as articulators of our connection to the sacred. The point of departure in this work for Heidegger is a poem by Rilke:

> As Nature gives the other creatures over
> to the venture of their dim delight
> and in soil and branchwork grants none special cover,
> so too our being's pristine ground settles our plight;
> we are no dearer to it; it ventures us.
> Except that we, more eager than plant or beast,
> go with this venture, will it, adventurous
> more sometimes than Life itself is, more daring
> by a breath (and not in the least
> from selfishness).... There, outside all caring,
> this creates for us a safety—just there,
> where the pure forces' gravity rules; in the end,
> it is our unshieldedness on which we depend,
> and that, when we saw it threaten, we turned it
> so into the Open that, in widest orbit somewhere,
> where the Law touches us, we may affirm it.[132]

Humanity enters into nature differently than animals or plants. Plants and animals become a part of nature's world, "the Open," without either any special protection or any worry. They live their lives the best they can in accord with their natural capacities, taking what nature has to offer as given. Humanity gains no special protection from the vagaries of nature, but rejects accepting nature as it stands:

> Man places before himself the world as the whole of everything objective, and he places himself before the world. Man sets up the world toward himself, and delivers Nature over to himself. Man produces new things where they are lacking to him. Man transposes things where they are in his way. [133]

We work hard to defy our vulnerability to the forces of nature, our "unshieldeness," but in the end nature's "Law" touches us and we too necessarily enter into the Open, as do all plants and animals:

> What is it that remains blocked off, withdrawn from us by ourselves in our ordinary willing to objectify the world? It is the other draft: Death. Death is what touches mortals in their nature, and so sets them on their way to the other side of life, and so into the whole of the pure draft. Death thus gathers into the whole of what is already posited, into the positum of the whole draft. Our unshieldedness, so converted, finally shelters us within the Open, outside all protection. [134]

We can build our own artificial world of encircling things to insulate us from exposure to earthly elements, but in the end we must obey the ultimate law of nature, that our life will come to an end and our material self will enter another form of being.

Heidegger can be accused of nostalgically looking backwards to a time when our connection with nature was more spiritually suffused and our life was guided by a sacred connection to the whole of Being, including mortals (our human selves), Earth and sky (nature), and the divinities. The divinities we created to mark out the sacred, death was seen as a part of life, and Earth and sky was our place of dwelling. His presumptions about our connection to nature lack the trappings of science, but they do appeal to the poetry within us. We moderns look to technology as our final source of power and stimulation, but our world of perception lacks mystery and a sacred quality. The power of the material attracts us, but there is nothing spiritual or mystifying in it. Is creating an Ipad with greater photographic resolution our essential purpose in life? Technology is little help in dealing with something only poets have a capacity to address—reconciliation of our life of wonder with an ultimate descent into suffering and death. Technology is a bull in a global China shop, breaking up what is sacred. This doesn't mean we should become Luddites, but it does infer that we should take technology in hand and use it more humbly and with greater sensitivity to the marvels of life and nature.

We in the modern world have become so accustomed to looking at everything as a utilitarian object, a something that will do something for us, that we have forgotten how amazing the presence of anything from a rock, to a space station, to a polar bear actually is. In his essay, "The Thing," Heidegger seeks to restore the mystery and wonder of any being, including those we humans bring into existence, such as ceramic jugs for storing wine or water. A jug, once made and set free to be what it is, has a self-supporting nature and takes on a life of its own:

> The making, it is true, lets the jug come into its own. But that which in the jug's nature is its own is never brought about by its making. Now released from the making process, the self-supporting jug has to gather itself for the task of containing. In the process of its making, of course, the jug must first show its outward appearance to the maker. But what shows itself here, the aspect (the eidos, the idea), characterizes the jug solely in the respect in which the vessel stands over against the maker as something to be made.[135]

The maker brings forth the jug using the fruits of the earth, but once made the jug stands as a free thing with a form and function of its own.

In the course of daily events, we take little time to ponder what a thing, such as a ceramic jug, actually is and does. Heidegger helps on this score in his own description of a jug's gift-giving role:

> How does the jug's void hold? It holds by taking what is poured in. It holds by keeping and retaining what it took in. The void holds in a twofold manner: taking and

keeping. The word 'hold' is therefore ambiguous. Nevertheless, the taking of what is poured in and the keeping of what was poured belong together. But their unity is determined by the outpouring for which the jug is fitted as a jug. The twofold holding of the void rests on the outpouring. In the outpouring, the holding is authentically how it is. To pour from the jug is to give...The giving of the outpouring can be a drink. The outpouring gives water, it gives wine to drink.[136]

This description casts a special light on the ordinary, and shows us what an amazing gift an ordinary thing actually is. My habitual cup of espresso each morning represents all the components of my being in the world. Earth and sky, the basic materials of nature, combine in both the cup that holds the espresso and in the coffee that is gifted to me. The mortals who are the agents of this combining, the barista, the coffee grower, and many more, enter into the espresso I drink as well. They, in effect, offer some of their being to me. That all that goes into my morning espresso exists in the first place is tinged with what I would call a sacred mystery. Here is where I would say Heidegger's divinities reside, in the mystery and wonder of beings themselves. What a privilege it is to enjoy a cup of espresso each morning.

We don't think consciously very often about how a jug or any other thing fits in the larger pattern of being, and our master guide to Being helps us out on that score:

The spring stays on in the water of the gift. In the spring the rock dwells, and in the rock dwells the dark slumber of the earth, which receives the rain and dew of the sky. In the water of the spring dwells the marriage of sky and earth. It stays in the wine given by the fruit of the vine, the fruit in which the earth's nourishment and the sky's sun are betrothed to one another. In the gift of water, in the gift of wine, sky and Earth dwell. But the gift of the outpouring is what makes the jug a jug. In the jugness of the jug, sky and Earth dwell. The gift of the pouring out is drink for mortals. It quenches their thirst. It refreshes their leisure. It enlivens their conviviality. But the jug's gift is at times also given for consecration. If the pouring is for consecration, then it does not still a thirst. It stills and elevates the celebration of the feast. The gift of the pouring now is neither given in an inn nor is the poured gift a drink for mortals. The outpouring is the libation poured out for the immortal gods. The gift of the outpouring as libation is the authentic gift. In giving the consecrated libation, the pouring jug occurs as the giving gift. The consecrated libation is what our word for a strong outpouring flow, 'gush,' really designates: gift and sacrifice.[137]

It's easy to get depressed about the pains and horrors of daily life after reading the morning paper, but the offset is contemplation like Heidegger's about a jug. He lost his way for a time with his attraction to Nazism, but his late writings offer to us an inspiring metaphysic for the sacredness of all beings. Hard nosed philosophers looking for a scientifically rigorous explanation of Being won't be satisfied with what they find in his constructions. Nonetheless, if we just take time to look and think as in "The Thing," the simplest of entities in our daily life possess a capacity to amaze us.

We don't need to become Luddites to appreciate the beauties and interests we find within our world of perception. Scientific explanations of causalities needn't trump a spiritual sense operating along with a pragmatic view about how we get through life. A life infused with spiritual concern for the whole of Being doesn't mean giving up our material comforts and pleasures, but it does suggest that we should give more attention to the impacts we have on the earth. A spiritual sense about the world we live in will push us, I conjecture, toward a more compact form of life that brings with it climate stability and more room for the rest of nature.

***

Let's step back from our Heideggerian poetic form of philosophizing (which is a bit much for my economist side anyway), and review trends already in place leading us in the direction of a more environmentally friendly form of life, and let's consider specifically the role a new spiritual turn could play in this.

Nietzsche's proclamation about the death of God, even if confined to Christianity, today looks premature. While traditional Christian institutions face declining public involvement, evangelical Christianity is on the rise worldwide, especially in Latin America, Africa, and East Asia. Similarly, Islam, a close cousin of Christianity, continues to expand its global reach. But in Europe and the U.S., participation in organized religion is on the wane, especially among the young. No matter their age, younger generations of Americans and Europeans engage less than older in formal religious activities, indicating that generational replacement will lead to an inexorable future decline of traditional religion in the U.S. and Europe. Globally, God is doing well in the religious marketplace so far, especially the Evangelical Christian and Islamic God, but not so much in the affluent West. Evangelicals have expanded their foothold in the U.S., but even their surge may be peaking. God may not be dead, but if the U.S. and Europe give us a glimpse of the future, commitment to monotheistic religion may be in trouble over the long haul.[138]

The death of God is not the same as a death of spirituality. Growing numbers who are unattached to any formal religion claim to still be "spiritual." Spirituality in the monotheistic mold pretty much meant a felt desire to venerate and treat as sacred a transcendent and all powerful divinity who resides beyond the world we see. A new kind of spirituality, gaining ground in Europe and the U.S. especially, looks to humanity and the world at hand for attachments to the sacred. Spiritual connection is to the inner-self, to life, or to existence as a whole. In short, life and beings intrinsically possess a spiritual sense pantheistic in its nature. Meaning comes from the deep recesses of the inner-self, not from an external, institutionally formed divine power. In short, the new world of spirituality and the sacred is self-creative and focuses on life as we experience it and the beings of the world.[139]

The content of this new kind of spirituality has yet to be properly nailed down by academics, and this is reflected in in the terminology of recent writings on the topic. Unaffiliated or private religiosity is a term used by some researchers who attempt to measure the phenomenon, applying the language of conventional organized religion to those who express spirituality but lack any direct involvement with a religious institution. Those who are privately religious don't attend church but believe in God, or some spiritual force, or engage in some form of religious behavior such as prayer. In Sweden, a country that ranks high in the possession of post-materialist values, the proportion of those who never attend church has been trending upwards to more than half, while those who occasionally attend has been declining. Frequent attenders stand at a relatively stable 10 percent of the population. Being privately religious and praying frequently correlates with post-materialist desires for nuclear free zones, an ecological society, public libraries, foreign aid, and refugee asylum, although this group tends to be pro-life in the question of abortion. Those who pray occasionally also express support for some post-materialist values at statistically significant levels, but being privately religious without active prayer fails to correlate with any post-materialist values. The intensely privately religious in Sweden, who engage in frequently in prayer, support an ecological society that protects the environment, a value of special interest to us here. The sample behind this correlation includes those born prior to World War II, baby boomers, and members of Generation X (born 1965-1979). The correlation of support for an ecological society and the intensely privately religious is due entirely to Generation X and doesn't extend to prior generations. Simply put, those who are young and intense in their private religious beliefs are more likely than others to express concern for the natural world.[140]

The new spiritual turn manifests itself publicly in the form of what has come to be know as the "New Age" movement not just in places like Sweden, but in most western countries, including Europe, the U.S., and Canada. This movement goes well beyond a traditional religiosity, private or otherwise, and includes a variety cf beliefs and practices ranging from meditation and a veneration of nature to reincarnation and astrology. Its central premise, if there is one, is that many pathways exist to spirituality. New Age spirituality looks inward to self-reflection instead of to an external transcendent sacred being. Rather than being external to one's life, the divine is within the world of our experience. A recent study of 14 western countries using the World Values Survey addressed the underlying reasons for the spiritual turn, identifying those who adhere to a "New Age," post-Christian spirituality as believers in some sort of spirit or life force but not a "personal God," believers in life after death who think that churches fail to satisfy spiritual needs, believers in reincarnation but not in God, or individuals who do not belong to a religious denomination or have much faith in churches and are not convinced atheists. Survey respondents who score highly on any of these descriptions fill the bill for belief in a post-Christian form of spirituality, and by this definition post-Christian spirituality has recently expanded the most in the Netherlands, Belgium, the U.S., and Ireland, and is highest in France, Great Britain, the Netherlands, and Sweden.[141]

The turn to a post-Christian spirituality in this study, according to statistical analysis, is driven by rising adherence to post-traditional values such as post-materialism (as defined by Inglehart), rejection of a strict hierarchical relationship between parent and child and between males and females, and openness to different forms of sexual behavior. The rise of post-Christian spirituality correlates with belonging to younger generations and with higher levels of educational achievement. In short, post-materialists, post-traditionalists, the young, and the well educated lie behind the trend to a post-Christian spirituality in western countries.

To describe the rise of post-Christian spirituality as strictly equivalent to a "New Age" movement, which involves some combination of belief in reincarnation, astrology, contact with the dead, and fortune telling, can be misleading. Unsurprisingly, "New Age" defined narrowly is not the only form that a post-Christian spirituality takes, and many who claim to be spiritual reject New Age tenants and focus instead on the sacredness of life and being itself and find their objects of veneration in the natural world.

A Norwegian statistical study offers interesting insights into the divide between adherents of New Age spiritual values and a self-constructed, individualized, meditative spirituality. Members of the later group orient themselves to living in harmony with their values, practicing meditation, and seeking a deeper meaning and a richer spirituality in their lives. By contrast, New Agers adhere to a strict beliefs in some combination of reincarnation, contact with the dead, astrology, and fortune telling. Self-constructed spirituality correlates positively with egalitarianism, post-materialism, and political ecology, while New Age values correlate negatively with post-materialism and political ecology and positively with a fatalist outlook. Norwegian New Agers lack veneration of the natural environment in their opposition to political ecology, but Norwegian spiritual self-constructers support of political ecology infers that some among them may well adhere to the idea of nature as a sacred entity.[142]

New Agers in the U.S. possess a different attitude toward the natural environment than their Norwegian counterparts, with self-described members of the movement in one local U.S. study commonly seeing the natural world as containing a spiritual significance. The sponginess of the term "New Age" may in part account for differences between the Norwegian and U.S. study, but there does seem to be a real difference in outlook as well. In the U.S., a sample of attendees at new age events who were later interviewed positively connect environmental concern to their spirituality, and support the idea that nature possesses an inner spiritual force. This attitude is at variance with the Norwegian New Age opposition to a political ecology.[143]

Oddly, a large sample of the conventionally religious in the U.S., including evangelicals, Catholics, and mainline protestants, express negative views about protecting the environment as opposed to the rest of the public who express positive views. Liberals and Democrats who fall in the conventionally religious camp support environmental protection, but their numbers are not large enough to offset the rest. The conventionally religious tend to be politically conservative and lack a positive view of environmental protection, and, conversely, those who don't engage in conventional religious activity favor environmental protection.[144]

A recent Australian study mirrors the U.S. result in its report on a specific instance where the religiously unaffiliated favor efforts to protect natural landscapes. Support for protecting old-growth forests in the country's southwest took a substantial leap as young, religiously unaffiliated, well educated individuals moved into the area. The study notes that those who recreate in such forestlands often find big old trees spiritually inspiring. This young and well educated demographic likely includes post-materialists oriented to an earth-based, as opposed to a more conventionally transcendent, spirituality.[145]

In sum, this evidence points to a connection between alternative spirituality and environmental protection among the young who are more predisposed than older generations to post-materialist values. A new spiritual turn looks to be a part of the explanation for a historical rise in support for protecting the natural environment.

***

I exercise frequently by climbing up and down a set of stairs connecting the top of a bluff with a beach on Lake Michigan. I could accomplish the same goal by using exercise machines at a gym, but it wouldn't be the same. I am especially taken on the stairs with light emerging through clouds, reflecting off the lake, making the snow sparkle in winter, turning the sand a bright white in the summer on a cloudless day, warming my face in below freezing winter temperatures, or turning the sky red at sunrise. On the stairs looking out over the lake, I feel amazed by the mystery of light. I am an atheist, but at such moments, I look at my surroundings with a special regard. The light and all that it reveals takes on an a unique wonder, and I begin to understand how one can see nature in spiritual terms. As an economist who studies human functioning in a material world, I never thought I would ever worry about the phenomenon of spirituality, but I am beginning to see why it is worth considering, especially if it takes up an earthly as opposed to a heavenly residence.

In his most famous writing, *Sand County Almanac*, Aldo Leopold proposes that a "...land ethic simply enlarges the boundary of the [human] community to include soils, waters, plants, and animals, or collectively: the land." Leopold also claims that "We can be ethical only in relation to something we can see, feel, understand, love, or otherwise have faith in." Putting these two ideas together with a growing post-material spiritual concern for the earth, the emergence of a deeply and widely held environmental ethic seems like a concrete possibility. With a spiritual turn towards the Earth and away from the heavens, the chance for us forming a bond with the human and natural world around us increases. If it is life on Earth that truly matters, our affections are more likely to flow toward both humanity and nature itself, and earthly beings will gain prominence in our personal circles of ethical concern. This is what Aldo Leopold is talking about. Anyone curious about how one man formed a special philosophical connection with the natural world   should take a look at *A Sand County Almanac*.[146]

***

Martin Heidegger in his post-war years expressed no love for technology, which he saw as having a logic of its own that separates humanity from a more natural connection to the Earth and its beings. In this book, we have already covered the details of Heidegger's critique and don't need to repeat them. In brief, humanity becomes enthralled with the power of technology and the amazing things it can create from the energy and raw materials of nature. In the process, technology comes to rule our way of life. We are the makers, adopters, and guides of technology, but we are caught up in its history. We may love technology, or hate it, but we didn't choose it. It's the legacy of a huge collective web of unplanned individual historical acts, each guided by a metaphysical outlook that sees nature in mathematical and utilitarian terms, that determined the course of technology's history.

The question for us, is what will happen to our relationship with technology going forward? Should we become Luddites and reject technology, or should we embrace it and shape it to fit a more ecologically friendly and humane connection to our earthly environment and all its beings? Heidegger suggests that the technology cow is out of the barn, and we can't get it back in. The only real option is to expand our horizons and take technology in hand instead of allowing it to dominate us. We need to move our working assumption—that science-based technology drives all—into a subordinate position where instead it becomes a simple tool for protecting nature's wonders and advancing humanity's creative impulses. In doing this, we become the stewards of beings, not their exploiters, and our essential joy is to experience the continuous revealing and unfolding of Being's mystery. In short, we should become true post-materialists.

Easier said than done, many would say, but all that we have discussed in these pages gives us hints about how the process of taking technology in hand could unfold. Heidegger's seeming fatalism about prospects for overcoming the human addiction to a consumption-driven materialist technology leaves open a small window of opportunity for bringing the technology bull to heal. Nietzsche-like free-spirited inventors of new values may not be able to individually change society's direction, but by going against the grain and choosing to live differently, they provide evidence that an alternative form of being in the world is distinctly possible, evidence of which may attract converts. Such a "demonstration effect" is exactly what marketers hope for to get consumers to buy a new style of running shoe or a new fancy wrist watch. Through the same kind of process, young post-materialist self-expressers, adopting a new, more interesting style of living, might just cumulatively alter political, social, and economic arrangements over the long haul.

We have already described a number of real world examples where individuals and groups move beyond conventional materialist goals to serve both personal and social ends. Young professionals, seeking to satisfy post-materialist values, lead a trend toward compact urban living. Artists and performers, who struggle to make ends meet, are revitalizing modest income, older neighborhoods in American cities, and are often suppliers of the experiences and products desired by the urbanizing young professional as well as suburban expat empty nesters, people who want to live close to downtown in order to have access to the cultural, artistic, and culinary experiences that city centers have to offer. A secondary virtue of living more compactly, as we have repeatedly emphasize, is a reduction in fossil fuel consumption in comparison with a low-density suburban form of life.

In many of the culturally conservative developing countries of the world, the shift to post-materialism is just getting started, yet trends toward the acceptance of certain post-material values are evident, especially in cases of environmentally friendly economic innovation. One of the most impressive of these is Ibrahim Abouleish's creation of Sekem organic farms in the Egyptian desert, a project he undertook in response to environmental degradation he observed in Nile Valley croplands and out of a desire to provide economic and cultural opportunities for rural Egyptians. In carrying out his work, Abouleish continued his lifelong commitment to the Muslim faith while at the same time pursuing environmental improvement using ecologically sustainable methods for growing and processing organic foods, pharmaceuticals, and cotton clothing and giving his employees opportunities for a decent income, access to education and health care, and creative self-expression. A young social entrepreneur with a post-materialist outlook, Sherif Hosny, left a successful career in a large multinational corporation to create Schaduf Urban Microfarms whose purpose is to improve the lives of Cairo's low income residence through the installation of rooftop hydroponic gardens where leafy green vegetables are raised for sale in local markets. A similar story can be told about Ahmed Zahran who left a promising career at Shell Oil in London to help start KarmSolar, a business with a vision of greening the desert using solar powered drip irrigation, water purification, and desalination systems. These are examples of social invention outside of government in the private business world undertaken to achieve social ends along with earning an adequate income.

Social invention is not necessarily confined to private business. DESERTEC, a nonprofit foundation, has put together an innovative plan to create thermal solar plants in the desert that can provide clean power for North Africa, the Middle East, and much of Europe, allowing that part of the world to get unhooked from fossil fuels while creating substantial economic opportunities in countries like Tunisia and Egypt. This plan serves as a foundation for actual, on the ground solar development in Tunisia and elsewhere, and is gaining adherents in both businesses and governments throughout Europe, the Middle East, and North Africa.

Governments too at times undertake inventive new approaches to solving social and environmental problems. The United Nations Environmental Program wrote a feasibility study for the installation of solar powered rooftop heaters in Tunisia that caught the Tunisian government's eye and led to the creation of the Prosol program that has installed hundreds of heaters saving the Tunisian government huge amounts of money on fossil fuel subsidies and moving the country in the direction of a clean and sustainable energy system. Egypt and other countries are looking to Prosol as a model for water heating in low income urban neighborhoods where water is now often heated dangerously and at the cost of human health using kerosene.

These are a few examples of social invention rooted in post-materialist motivations that can help create green and prosperous economies in North Africa and the Middle East. This will not happen easily until the transitions to democracy, another post-materialist value, gain full traction, which, judging by recent events, will take some time. Meanwhile, in cities like Cairo innovations continue in the informal economy outside of the bureaucratic and oppressive state apparatus left over from the days of dictatorship. The most amazing accomplishment of all is the creation of one of the world's most compact cities with well-constructed housing by Egyptian families themselves using their own meager finances and efforts despite governmental barriers. With a democratically controlled public sector supplying efficient mass transit, quality basic municipal services, and increased green space, Cairo's future prospects for being a compact, environmentally friendly, and energy efficient city would be vastly improved. What the future actually holds, only time will tell.

As we can see in all these examples, technology is integral to the advancement of larger social purposes. Strictly materialist ends get reshaped and modified, and those technologies that promote a more just and environmentally friendly life take center stage. Humanity here drives technology, not the other way around, and taking technology in hand for social ends gains a fuller sway when post-materialist values become more prevalent, even in the context of Islam, as Ibrahim Abouleish has shown us in his work at Sekem.

I would like to end with some parting comments inspired by Martin Heidegger's piece entitled "The Question Concerning Technology," a work anyone worried about the fate of the Earth should read.[147]

His message here suggests that we need to look more closely at the role of technology in our modern life, and if we do this with care and discernment, we will see what we are missing. The modern norm is to view nature in strictly instrumental terms as a pile of resources available for our material exploitation, a "standing reserve" as Heidegger puts it. This is exactly how we, in our role as pure materialists, "enframe," or box in, the natural world outside our human skin. We also look at bringing forth technical marvels from "standing reserves" as an engineering problem to be solved without giving serious attention to the needs of humanity for creative action and meaning. In short, we "enframe" humanity as a tool to be blended with "standing reserves" for the purpose of serving the consumer economy where the acquisition of material possessions rules. Our enthrallment with the technological distracts us from the mystery and wonder of beings in both the natural realm and the arena of human social action and connection. If only the goods of the market are important to us, then we want these without much attention to consequences. We place nature and humanity in a box of production and do what is necessary to get the most material possessions out of it. If we wonder at the marvels that unfold in nature and from humanity itself, then we will desire to protect both from technological ravishment. Instead of building huge dams and coal fired power plants that destroy nature's unfolding and self-revealings, we will construct solar energy panels and wind generators and place them where their harms to nature and humanity will be at a minimum. Instead of cranking out more and more marketable possessions, we will arrange production of material goods to minimize human harm and tedium and to maximize the exercise of human creativity, and we will choose what we produce and buy in compliance with true human flourishing. Finally, we will choose our mode of living to leave sufficient space for the rest of nature so that it can evolve and change according to its own inner dynamic.

This is my interpretation of what Heidegger is telling us in "The Question Concerning Technology" and where, I think, post-materialists are heading. To get unhooked from rule by materialist premises and move to a poetic attachment to all earthly beings calls for a change in our philosophical outlook, which I would say has a pretty good chance of happening in a post-materialist world. Let's take technology in hand to save the Earth and give our own lives greater meaning in the process.

Bibliography

Abouleish, Ibrahim. *Sekem: A Sustainable Community in the Egyptian Desert*. Edinburgh: Floris Books, 2005.

Abouleish, Ibrahim, and Helmy Abouleish. "Garden in the Desert: Sekem Makes Comprehensive Sustainable Development a Reality ". *Innovations* 3 (2008): 21-48.

Albers, Ronald, and Marga Peeters. "Food and Energy Prices, Government Subsidies and Fiscal Balances in South Mediterranean Countries." In *Economics Paper 437*. Brussels, 2011.

Alesina, Alberto, Edward Glaeser, and Bruce Sacerdote. "Work and Leisure in the United States and Europe: Why So Different?". Chap. 1 In *NBER Macroeconomics Annual 2005*, edited by Mark Gertler and Kenneth Rogoff. Cambridge: MIT Press, 2005.

Alper, Neil O., and Gregory H. Wassall. "Artists' Careers and Their Labor Markets." Chap. 23 In *Handbook of the Economics of Art and Culture*, edited by Victor A. Ginsburgh and David Throsby. Amsterdam: North-Holland, 2006.

Beckers, Tilo, Pascal Siegers, and Anabel Kuntz. "Congruence and Performance of Value Concepts in Social Research." *Survey Research Methods* 6 (2012): 13-24.

Birch, Eugenie L. "Who Lives Downtown?". Washington D.C.: Brookings Institution, 2005.

Bloch, Jon P. "Alternative Spirituality and Environmentalism." *Review of Religion Research* 40 (1998): 55-73.

Booth, Douglas E. *The Coming Good Boom: Creating Prosperity for All and Saving the Environment through Compact Living*. Charleston: Create Space, 2010.

— — —. *Hooked on Growth: Economic Addictions and the Environment.* Lanham: Rowman & Littlefield, 2004.

Botvar, Pal Ketil. "Alternative Religion – a New Political Cleavage?: An Analysis of Norwegian Survey Data on New Forms of Spirituality." *Politics and Religion* 2 (2009): 378-94.

Chandler, Siobhan. "The Social Ethic of Religiously Unaffiliated Spirituality." *Religious Compass* 2 (2008): 240-56.

Dasgupta, Susmita, Benoit Laplante, Craig Meisner, David Wheeler, and Jianping Yan. "The Impact of Sea Level Rise on Developing Countries: A Comparative Analysis." In *Working Paper 4136.* Washington D.C.: World Bank, 2007.

DESERTEC Foundation. "Clean Power from Deserts: The Desertec Concept for Energy, Water and Climate Security." In *WhiteBook.* Bonn: DESERTEC Foundation, 2009.

— — —. "Desertec Milestones." http://www.desertec.org/global-mission/milestones/.

Detrie, Megan. "'Schaduf' Sets up Rooftop Urban Farms for Low-Income Families." *Egypt Independent,* March 16, 2012.

Diener, Ed, and Robert Biswas-Diener. "Will Money Increase Subjective Well-Being?: A Literature Review and Guide to Needed Research." *Social Indicators Research* 37 (2009): 119-54.

Diener, Ed, Richard E. Lucas, and Christie Napa Scollon. "Beyond the Hedonic Treadmill: Revising the Adaptation Theory of Well-Being." *Social Indicators Research* 37 (2009): 103-18.

Diener, Ed, and Martin Seligman. "Beyond Money: Toward an Economy of Well-Being." *Social Indicators Research Series* 37 (2009): 201-65.

Dietz, Thomas, An Stirling Frisch, Paul C. Stern, and Grego Guagnano. "Values and Vegetarianism: An Exploratory Analysis." *Rural Sociology* 60 (1995): 533-42.

Duquennois, Anne Nicole, and Peter Newman. "Linking the Green and Brown Agendas: A Case Study on Cairo, Egypt." In *Revisiting Urban Planning: Global Report on Human Settlements 2009*, 2009.

Edwards, Douglas. *I'm Feeling Lucky: The Confessions of Google Employee Number 59*. New York: Houghton Mifflin, 2011.

El-Batran, Manal, and Christian Arandel. "A Shelter of Their Own: Informal Settlement Expansion in Greater Cairo and Government Responses." *Environment and Urbanization* 10 (1998): 217-32.

FAO. "The State of Food and Agriculture." Rome: Food and Agricultural Organization of the United Nations, 2009.

Feuer, Alan. "On the Move, in a Thriving Tech Sector." *New York Times* November 19, 2011.

Florida, Richard. *The Rise of the Creative Class: And How It's Transforming Work, Leisure, Community and Everyday Life*. New York: Basic Books, 2002.

Foundation, DESERTEC. "Clean Power from Deserts: The Desertec Concept for Energy, Water and Climate Security." In *WhiteBook*. Bonn: DESERTEC Foundation, 2009.

Franzen, A., and R. Meyer. "Environmental Attitudes in Cross-National Perspective: A Multilevel Analysis of the ISSP 1993 and 2000." *European Sociological Review* 26, no. 2 (2009): 219-34.

Garhammer, Manfred. "Pace and Enjoyment of Life." *Journal of Happiness Studies* 3 (2002): 217-56.

Gelissen, John. "Explaining Popular Support for Environmental Protection: A Multilevel Analysis of 50 Nations." *Environment and Behavior* 39, no. 3 (2007): 392-415.

Genc, Yusif, Julie Hayes, and Yuri Shavrukov. "Hydroponics - a Standard Methodology for Plant Biological Researches." ResearchGate, http://www.researchgate.net/publication/233927805_Hydroponics_-

_A_Standard_Methodology_for_Plant_Biological_R esearches?ev=pub_srch_pub.

Gerbens-Leenes, P.W., and S. Nonhebel. "Consumption Patterns and Their Effects on Land Required for Food." *Ecological Economics* 42 (2002): 185-99.

Gerhards, Jurgen, and Holger Lengfeld. "Support for European Union Environmental Policy by Citizens of Eu-Member and Accession States." *Comparative Sociology* 7 (2008): 1-27.

Gilbert, Daniel. *Stumbling on Happiness.* New York: Knopf, 2006.

Givens, J. E., and A. K. Jorgenson. "The Effects of Affluence, Economic Development, and Environmental Degradation on Environmental Concern: A Multilevel Analysis." *Organization & Environment* 24, no. 1 (2011): 74-91.

Gruber, Jonathan, and Brigitte C. Madrian. "Health Insurance, Labor Supply, and Job Mobility: A Critical Review of the Literature." In *Working Paper 8817.* Cambridge: National Bureau of Economic Research, 2002.

Guth, James L., John C. Green, Lyman A. Kellstedt, and Corwin E. Smidt. "Faith and the Environment: Religious Beliefs and Attitudes on Environmental Policy." *American Journal of Political Science* 39 (1995): 364-82.

Hagevi, Magnus. "Beyond Church and State: Private Religiosity and Post-Materialist Political Opinion among Individuals in Sweden." *Journal of Church and State* 54 (2012): 499-525.

Hayden, A. "Work-Time Reduction and the Dutch Economic Miracle." Toronto: 32 Hours: Action for Full Employment, 1999.

Heidegger, Martin. *Being and Time.* Translated by John Macquarrie and Edward Robinson. Oxford: Blackwell, 1962.

———. "Building Dwelling Thinking." In *Martin Heidegger: Basic Writings*, edited by David Farrell Krell. 343-64. San Francisco: Harper, 1992.

— — —. "The Origin of the Work of Art." In *Martin Heidegger: Basic Writings*, edited by David Farrell Krell. 139-212. San Francisco: Harper, 1992.

— — —. "The Question Concerning Technology." In *Martin Heidegger: Basic Writings*, edited by David Farrell Krell. 307-42. San Francisco: Harper, 1992.

— — —. "The Thing." Translated by Albert Hofstader. Chap. 5 In *Poetry, Language, Thought*. New York: Harper & Row, 2001.

— — —. "What Are Poets For?" Translated by Albert Hofstader. Chap. 3 In *Poetry, Language, Thought*. New York: Harper & Row, 2001.

— — —. *What Is Called Thinking?* Translated by J. Glenn Gray. New York: Harper, 1976.

Hoogendoorn, Brigitte, and Chantal Hartog. "Prevalence and Determinants of Social Entrepreneurshp at the Macro-Level." In *EIM Research Reports*. Zoetermeer: Panteia/EIM, 2011.

Houtman, Dick, and Stef Aupers. "The Spiritual Turn and the Decline of Tradition: The Spread of Post-Christian Spirituality in 14 Western Countries, 1981–2000." *Journal for the Scientific Study of Religion* 46 (2007): 305-20.

Inglehart, Ronald F. "Changing Values among Western Publics from 1970 to 2006." *West European Politics* 31, no. 1-2 (2008): 130-46.

— — —. "Public Support for Environmental Protection: Objective Problems and Subjective Values in 43 Societies." *Political Science and Politics* 28 (1995): 57-72.

— — —. "The Worldviews of Islamic Publics in Global Perspective." Chap. 2 In *Values and Perceptions of the Islamic and Middle Eastern Publics*, edited by Mansoor Moaddel. 25-46. New York: Palgrave, 2007.

Inglehart, Ronald F., and Paul R. Abramson. "Economic Security and Value Change." *American Political Science Review* 88 (1994): 336-54.

Inglehart, Ronald F., and Wayne E. Baker. "Modernization, Cultural Change, and the Persistence of Traditional Values." *American Sociological Review* 65 (2000): 19-51.

Kalof, Linda, Thomas Dietz, Paul C. Stern, and Gregory A. Guagnano. "Social Psychology and Structural Influences on Vegetarian Beliefs." *Rural Sociology* 64 (1999): 500-11.

Kenny, Judith T., and Jeffrey Zimmerman. "Constructing the 'Genuine American City': Neo-Traditionalism, New Urbanism and Neo-Liberalism in the Remaking of Downtown Milwaukee." *Cultural Geographies* 11 (2003): 74-98.

Kenworthy, J.R. "Transport Energy Use and Greenhouse Gases in Urban Passenger Transport Systems: A Study of 84 Global Cities." Murdoch, Western Australia: Murdoch University, 2003.

Kuhn, Randall. "On the Role of Human Development in the Arab Spring." Boulder: Institute of Behaviorial Science, University of Colorado, 2011.

Kvaloy, Berit, Henning Finseraas, and Ola Listhaug. "The Publics' Concern for Global Warming: A Cross-National Study of 47 Countries." *journal of Peace Research* 49 (2012): 11-22.

Leopold, Aldo. *A Sand County Almanac: With Essays on Conservation from Round River* New York: Ballantine Books, 1970.

Lloyd, Richard. *Neo-Bohemia: Art and Commerce in the Postindustrial City*. New York: Routledge, 2006.

―――. "Neo-Bohemia: Art and Neighborhood Redevelopment in Chicago." *Journal of Urban Affairs* 24 (2002): 517-32.

Markusen, Ann, and Greg Schrock. "The Artistic Dividend: Urban Artistic Specialisation and Economic Development Implications." *Urban Studies* 43, no. 10 (2006): 1661-86.

Mourshed, Mona. "Rethinking Irrigation Technology Adoption: Lessons from the Egyptian Desert." In

Working Paper Number 23, Program in Science, Technology, and Society. Cambridge: MIT, 1995.

Nawrotzki, Raphael. "The Politics of Environmental Concern: A Cross-National Analysis." *Organization & Environment* 25 (2012): 286-307.

Newport, Frank. "In U.S., 5% Consider Themselves Vegetarians." Gallup Wellbeing, http://www.gallup.com/poll/156215/consider-themselves-vegetarians.aspx.

Nickerson, Carol, Norbert Schwartz, Ed Diener, and Daniel Kahneman. "Zeroing in on the Dark Side of the American Dream: A Closer Look at the Negative Consequences of the Goal for Financial Success." *Psychological Science* 14 (2003): 531-36.

Nickerson, Carol, Norbert Schwarz, and Ed Diener. "Financial Aspirations, Financial Success, and Overall Life Satisfaction: Who? And How?". *Journal of Happiness Studies* 8, no. 4 (2007): 467-515.

Nietzsche, Friedrich. "Beyond Good and Evil: Prelude to a Philosophy of the Future." In *Basic Writings of Nietzsche*, edited by Walter Kaufmann. 179-436. New York: Random House, 2000.

———. "The Birth of Tragedy: Out of the Spirit of Music." In *Basic Writings of Nietzsche*, edited by Walter Kaufmann. 15-144. New York: Random House, 2000.

———. *The Dawn of Day*. Translated by J. M. Kennedy. London: Dover, 2007.

———. *The Gay Science*. Translated by Josefine Nauckhoff and Adrian Del Caro. Edited by Bernard Williams. Cambridge: Cambridge University Press, 2001.

———. *Human, All-Too-Human*. Translated by Helen Zimmern and Paul V. Cohn. Lawrence: Digireads.com, 2009.

———. *Thus Spoke Zarathustra: A Book for None and All*. Translated by Walter Kaufmann. New York: Penguin Books, 1978.

———. *Twilight of the Idols*. Oxford: Oxford University Press, 1998.

———. *Will to Power*. Translated by Anthony M. Ludovici. New York2006.

Okulicz-Kozaryn, Adam. "Europeans Work to Live and Americans Live to Work (Who Is Happy to Work More: Americans or Europeans." *Journal of Happiness Studies* 12 (2011): 225-43.

Olz, Samantha, and Lawrence Agbemabiese. "Innovative Energy Policy in a Developing Country Context: Experience from UNEP's Prosol Initiative." *Wiley Interdisciplinary Reviews: Energy and Environment* 1 (2012): 69-80.

Perkins, Harold A. "Green Spaces of Self-Interest within Shared Urban Governance." *Geography Compass* 4 (2010): 255-58.

Putnam, Robert D., and David E. Campbell. *American Grace: How Religion Divides and Unites Us*. New York: Simon & Schuster, 2010.

Reynolds, Jeremy. "You Can't Always Get the Hours You Want: Mismatches between Actual and Preferred Work Hours in the U.S." *Social Forces* 81, no. 4 (2003): 1171-99.

Rice, Gillian. "Pro-Environmental Behavior in Egypt: Is There a Role for Islamic Environmental Ethics?". *Journal of Business Ethics* 65, no. 4 (2006): 373-90.

Rorty, Richard. *Philosophy and Social Hope*. New York: Penquin, 1999.

Rusli, Evelyn M. "Zynga's Tough Culture Risks a Talent Drain." *New York Times*, November 11, 2011.

Sarant, Louise. "Renewable Energy Forum at the Arab League: On Regulations and Pan-Arabism." *Egypt Independent*, April 24, 2012.

Sartre, Jean-Paul. *Being and Nothingness*. New York: Washington Square Press, 1992.

———. *Nausea*. New York: New Directions, 2007.

Sengupta, Somini. "Reticent Rich: Preferred Style in Silicon Valley." *New York Times*, May 18, 2012, A1.

Shilad, Justin. "Can Local and Regional Projects Help Renewable Energy Go Mainstream?" *Egypt Independent*, December 12, 2012.

Sims, David. *Understanding Cairo: The Logic of a City out of Control.* Cairo: American University in Cairo Press, 2010.

Sirgy, M. Joseph, and Jiyun Wu. "The Pleasant Life, the Engaged Life, and the Meaningful Life: What About the Balanced Life?". *Journal of Happiness Studies* 10, no. 2 (2007): 183-96.

Sousa-Poza, Alfonso, and Adres A. Sousa-Poza. "Well-Being at Work: A Cross-National Analysis of the Level and Determinants of Job Satisfaction." *Journal of Socio-Economics* 29 (2000): 517-38.

Soussa, H.K. "Effects of Drip Irrigation Water Amount on Crop Yield, Productivity and Efficiency of Water Use in Desert Regions in Egypt." *Nile Basin Water Science & Engineering Journal* 3 (2010): 96-109.

Strom, E. "Artist Garret as Growth Machine? Local Policy and Artist Housing in U.S. Cities." *Journal of Planning Education and Research* 29, no. 3 (2010): 367-78.

Tessler, Mark. "Do Islamic Orientations Influence Attitudes toward Democracy in the Arab World? Evidence from the World Values Survey in Egypt, Jordan, Morocco, and Algeria." Chap. 5 In *Values and Perceptions of the Islamic and Middle Eastern Publics*, edited by Mansoor Moaddel. New York: Palgrave, 2007.

Tjernstrom, E., and T. Tietenberg. "Do Differences in Attitudes Explain Differences in National Climate Change Policies?". *Ecological Economics* 65 (2012): 315-24.

Tolan, Tom. *Riverwest: A Community History.* Milwaukee: Past Press, 2003.

Touhami, Myriem, and Ghita Hannane. "Prosol: Financing Solar Water Heating in Tunisia." United Nations Environment Programme, DTIE, http://

climatepolicyinitiative.org/wp-content/uploads/
2011/12/Touhami-and-Hannane_PROSOL.pdf.
Trabacchi, Chiara, Valerio Micale, and Gianleo Frisari.
"San Giorgio Group Case Study: Prosol Tunisia."
San Francisco: Climate Policy Initiaitve, 2012.
TuNur. "Tunur Project." TuNur Project, http://www.tunur.tn/.
Twitchell, James B. *Lead Us into Temptation: The Triumph
of the American Dream*. New York: Columbia
University Press, 1999.
Uhlaner, Lorraine, and Roy Thurik. "Postmaterialism
Influencing Total Entrepreneurial Activity across
Nations." *Journal of Evolutionary Economics* 17,
no. 2 (2007): 161-85.
United Nations Human Development Program (UNDP).
"International Human Development Indicators."
UNDP, http://hdr.undp.org/en/statistics/data/.
USDA. "Agricultural Fact Book, 2001-2002." edited by
Office of Communications US Department of
Agriculture. Washington D.C.: U.S. Government
Printing Office, 2003.
Viney, Steven. "Karmsolar Develops Renewable Energy
Solution for 'Off Grid' Farmers." *Egypt Indepedent*,
March 22, 2012.
Visser, Jelle. "The First Part-Time Economy in the World:
A Model to Be Followed?". *Journal of European
Social Policy* 12, no. 1 (2002): 23-42.
Wei, Max, Shana Patadia, and Daniel M. Kammen.
"Putting Renewables and Energy Efficiency to
Work: How Many Jobs Can the Clean Energy
Industry Generate in the U.S.?". *Energy Policy* 38
(2010): 919-31.
Welzel, Christian, and Ronald F. Inglehart. "The Role of
Ordinary People in Democratization." *Journal of
Democracy* 19 (2008): 126-40.
White, Thomas. "Diet and the Distribution of Environmental
Impact." *Ecological Economics* 34 (2000): 145-53.
World Bank. "Middle East and North Africa Region
Assessment of Local Manufacturing Potential for

Concentrating Solar Power (CSP) Projects."
Washington D.C.: World Bank, 2011.

Worth, David. "Our New Cathedrals: Spirituality and Old-Growth Forests in Western Australia." In, *Portal Journal of Multidisciplinary Studies* 3, (2006). http://epress.lib.uts.edu.au/journals/index.php/portal/article/view/124.

Yaros, Bernard. "Solar Power Initiative Could Make Egypt Power Source for Europe." *Tunisia LIve*, February 8, 2012.

Young, Julian. *Friedrich Nietzsche: A Philosophical Biography.* Cambridge: Cambridge University Press, 2010.

— — —. *Heidegger's Later Philosophy.* Cambridge: Cambridge University Press, 2002.

Zahran, Sammy, Eunyi Kim, Xi Chen, and Mark Lubell. "Ecological Development and Global Climate Change: A Cross-National Study of Kyoto Protocol Ratification." *Society & Natural Resources* 20, no. 1 (2007): 37-55.

Zimmerman, J. "From Brew Town to Cool Town: Neoliberalism and the Creative City Development Strategy in Milwaukee." *Cities* 25, no. 4 (2008): 230-42.

Notes

[1] Manfred Garhammer, "Pace and Enjoyment of LIfe," *Journal of Happiness Studies* 3(2002); Ed Diener, Richard E. Lucas, and Christie Napa Scollon, "Beyond the Hedonic Treadmill: Revising the Adaptation Theory of Well-Being," *Social Indicators Research* 37(2009); Ed Diener and Robert Biswas-Diener, "Will Money Increase Subjective Well-Being?: A Literature Review and Guide to Needed Research," *Social Indicators Research* 37(2009).

[2] M. Joseph Sirgy and Jiyun Wu, "The Pleasant Life, the Engaged Life, and the Meaningful Life: What about the Balanced Life?," *Journal of Happiness Studies* 10, no. 2 (2007).

[3] Diener and Biswas-Diener, "Will Money Increase Subjective Well-Being?: A Literature Review and Guide to Needed Research."

[4] Carol Nickerson, Norbert Schwarz, and Ed Diener, "Financial aspirations, financial success, and overall life satisfaction: who? and how?," *Journal of Happiness Studies* 8, no. 4 (2007); Carol Nickerson et al., "Zeroing in on the dark side of the American dream: A Closer Look at the Negative Consequences of the Goal for Financial Success," *Psychological Science* 14(2003).

[5] James B. Twitchell, *Lead Us into Temptation: The Triumph of the American Dream* (New York: Columbia University Press, 1999).

[6] Douglas E. Booth, *The Coming Good Boom: Creating Prosperity for All and Saving the Environment through Compact Living* (Charleston: Create Space, 2010). See Chapter 1.

[7] Douglas Edwards, *I'm Feeling Lucky: The Confessions of Google Employee Number 59* (New York: Houghton Mifflin, 2011).

[8]Ronald F. Inglehart and Paul R. Abramson, "Economic Security and Value Change," *American Political Science Review* 88(1994).

[9]For example, see Chum-chih Chang and Te-Sheng Chen, "Idealism versus Reality: Empirical Test of Postmaterialism in China and Taiwan," *Issues and Studies* 49, no. 2 (2013).

[10]Paul R. Abramson and Ronald F. Inglehart, *Value Change in Global Perspective* (Ann Arbor: University of Michigan Press, 1995); Inglehart and Abramson, "Economic Security and Value Change."

[11]Ronald F. Inglehart, "Changing Values among Western Publics from 1970 to 2006," *West European Politics* 31, no. 1-2 (2008).

[12]Ibid.; Inglehart and Abramson, "Economic Security and Value Change."

[13]Chang and Chen, "Idealism versus Reality: Empirical Test of Postmaterialism in China and Taiwan."

[14]Inglehart, "Changing Values among Western Publics from 1970 to 2006."; Inglehart and Abramson, "Economic Security and Value Change."; Christian Welzel and Ronald F. Inglehart, "The Role of Ordinary People in Democratization," *Journal of Democracy* 19(2008).

[15]Ronald F. Inglehart, "Public Support for Environmental Protection: Objective Problems and Subjective Values in 43 Societies," *Political Science and Politics* 28(1995).

[16]Inglehart, "Changing Values among Western Publics from 1970 to 2006."; Inglehart and Abramson, "Economic Security and Value Change."

[17]Shalom H. Schwartz, "Are There Universal Aspects in the Structure and Contents of Human Values?," *Journal of Social Issues* 50, no. 4 (1994).

[18]Tilo Beckers, Pascal Siegers, and Anabel Kuntz, "Congruence and Performance of Value Concepts in Social Research," *Survey Research Methods* 6(2012).

[19]Schwartz, "Are There Universal Aspects in the Structure and Contents of Human Values?."

[20]Dick Houtman and Stef Aupers, "The Spiritual Turn and the Decline of Tradition: The Spread of Post-Christian Spirituality in 14 Western Countries, 1981–2000," *Journal for the Scientific Study of Religion* 46(2007).

[21]Magnus Hagevi, "Beyond Church and State: Private Religiosity and Post-Materialist Political Opinion among Individuals in Sweden," *Journal of Church and State* 54 (2012).

[22]Pal Ketil Botvar, "Alternative Religion – A New Political Cleavage?: An Analysis of Norwegian Survey Data on New Forms of Spirituality," *Politics and Religion* 2(2009).

[23]Jonathan Haidt, *The Righteous Mind: Why Good People are Divided by Politics and Religion* (New York: Random House, 2012).

[24]Ronald F. Inglehart and Wayne E. Baker, "Modernization, Cultural Change, and the Persistence of Traditional Values," *American Sociological Review* 65(2000).

[25]Ronald F. Inglehart, "The Worldviews of Islamic Publics in Global Perspective," in *Values and Perceptions of the Islamic and Middle Eastern Publics*, ed. Mansoor Moaddel (New York: Palgrave, 2007).

[26] Randall Kuhn, "On the Role of Human Development in the Arab Spring," (Boulder: Institute of Behaviorial Science, University of Colorado, 2011).

[27] Friedrich Nietzsche, "The Birth of Tragedy: Out of the Spirit of Music," in *Basic Writings of Nietzsche*, ed. Walter Kaufmann (New York: Random House, 2000).

[28] Friedrich Nietzsche, *Human, All-Too-Human*, trans. Helen Zimmern and Paul V. Cohn (Lawrence: Digireads.com, 2009); Friedrich Nietzsche, *The Dawn of Day*, trans. J. M. Kennedy (London: Dover, 2007); Friedrich Nietzsche, *The Gay Science*, ed. Bernard Williams, trans. Josefine Nauckhoff and Adrian Del Caro (Cambridge: Cambridge University Press, 2001).

[29] Friedrich Nietzsche, *Thus Spoke Zarathustra: A Book for None and All*, trans. Walter Kaufmann (New York: Penguin Books, 1978).

[30] Nietzsche, "Beyond Good and Evil: Prelude to a Philosophy of the Future."

[31] Julian Young, *Friedrich Nietzsche: A Philosophical Biography* (Cambridge: Cambridge University Press, 2010).

[32] Friedrich Nietzsche, *Will to Power*, trans. Anthony M. Ludovici (New York2006).

[33] Young, *Friedrich Nietzsche: A Philosophical Biography*. See page 542. He expresses a similar sentiment in *Twilight of the Idols:* "I mistrust all systematizers and avoid them. The will to a system is a lack of integrity."

[34] Ibid. See pages 497-503; Friedrich Nietzsche, *Twilight of the Idols* (Oxford: Oxford University Press, 1998).

[35] Nietzsche, *Thus Spoke Zarathustra: A Book for None and All*.

[36] Martin Heidegger, *What is Called Thinking?* , trans. J. Glenn Gray (New York: Harper, 1976).

[37] Martin Heidegger, *Being and Time*, trans. John Macquarrie and Edward Robinson (Oxford: Blackwell, 1962).

[38] The remaining sections in this chapter owe much to the following work: Julian Young, *Heidegger's Later Philosophy* (Cambridge: Cambridge University Press, 2002).

[39] Martin Heidegger, "The Origin of the Work of Art," in *Martin Heidegger: Basic Writings*, ed. David Farrell Krell (San Francisco: Harper, 1992); Martin Heidegger, "The Question Concerning Technology," in *Martin Heidegger: Basic Writings*, ed. David Farrell Krell (San Francisco: Harper, 1992); Heidegger, "Building Dwelling Thinking."

[40] Ibid.

[41] Tom Tolan, *Riverwest: A Community History* (Milwaukee: Past Press, 2003); Harold A. Perkins, "Green Spaces of Self-Interest Within Shared Urban Governance," *Geography Compass* 4(2010); J. Zimmerman, "From brew town to cool town: Neoliberalism and the creative city development strategy in Milwaukee," *Cities* 25, no. 4 (2008).

[42] Richard Florida, *The Rise of the Creative Class: And How It's Transforming Work, Leisure, Community and Everyday LIfe* (New York: Basic Books, 2002).

[43] Eugenie L. Birch, "Who LIves Downtown?," (Washington D.C.: Brookings Institution, 2005).

[44] Zimmerman, "From brew town to cool town: Neoliberalism and the creative city development strategy in Milwaukee."; Judith T. Kenny and Jeffrey Zimmerman, "Constructing the 'Genuine American City': Neo-traditionalism, New Urbanism and Neo-Liberalism in the Remaking of Downtown Milwaukee," *Cultural Geographies* 11(2003).

[45] Booth, *The Coming Good Boom: Creating Prosperity for All and Saving the Environment through Compact Living*. Chapters 5-9.

[46] Ann Markusen and Greg Schrock, "The artistic dividend: Urban artistic specialisation and economic development implications," *Urban Studies* 43, no. 10 (2006).

[47] Ibid.; E. Strom, "Artist Garret as Growth Machine? Local Policy and Artist Housing in U.S. Cities," *Journal of Planning Education and Research* 29, no. 3 (2010).

[48] Neil O. Alper and Gregory H. Wassall, "Artists' Careers and their Labor Markets," in *Handbook of the Economics of Art and Culture*, ed. Victor A. Ginsburgh and David Throsby (Amsterdam: North-Holland, 2006).

[49] Richard Lloyd, *Neo-Bohemia: Art and Commerce in the Postindustrial City* (New York: Routledge, 2006).

[50] Ibid.; Richard Lloyd, "Neo-Bohemia: Art and Neighborhood Redevelopment in Chicago," *Journal of Urban Affairs* 24(2002).

[51] Tolan, *Riverwest: A Community History*.

[52] Jean-Paul Sartre, *Being and Nothingness* (New York: Washington Square Press, 1992).

[53] Jean-Paul Sartre, *Nausea* (New York: New Directions, 2007).

[54] Sartre, *Being and Nothingness*. Page 101.

[55] Lloyd, *Neo-Bohemia: Art and Commerce in the Postindustrial City*.

[56] Ibid.

[57] Tolan, *Riverwest: A Community History*.

[58] Ed Diener and Martin Seligman, "Beyond Money: Toward an Economy of Well-Being," *Social Indicators Research Series* 37(2009); Alfonso Sousa-Poza and Adres A. Sousa-Poza, "Well-Being at Work: A Cross-national Analysis of the Level and Determinants of Job Satisfaction," *Journal of Socio-Economics* 29(2000).

[59] Alan Feuer, "On the Move, in a Thriving Tech Sector," *New York Times* November 19, 2011.

[60] Evelyn M. Rusli, "Zynga's Tough Culture Risks a Talent Drain," *New York Times*, November 11, 2011.

[61] Sousa-Poza and Sousa-Poza, "Well-Being at Work: A Cross-national Analysis of the Level and Determinants of Job Satisfaction."

[62] Florida, *The Rise of the Creative Class: And How It's Transforming Work, Leisure, Community and Everyday LIfe*.

[63] Jeremy Reynolds, "You Can't Always Get the Hours You Want: Mismatches between Actual and Preferred Work Hours in the U.S," *Social Forces* 81, no. 4 (2003).

[64] Daniel Gilbert, *Stumbling on Happiness* (New York: Knopf, 2006). Page 221.

[65] Alberto Alesina, Edward Glaeser, and Bruce Sacerdote, "Work and Leisure in the United States and Europe: Why So Different?," in *NBER Macroeconomics Annual 2005*, ed. Mark Gertler and Kenneth Rogoff (Cambridge: MIT Press, 2005).

[66] Adam Okulicz-Kozaryn, "Europeans Work to Live and Americans Live to Work (Who is Happy to Work More: Americans or Europeans," *Journal of Happiness Studies* 12(2011).

196

67 Jonathan Gruber and Brigitte C. Madrian, "Health Insurance, Labor Supply, and Job Mobility: A Critical Review of the Literature," in *Working Paper 8817* (Cambridge: National Bureau of Economic Research, 2002).

68 Alper and Wassall, "Artists' Careers and their Labor Markets."

69 A. Hayden, "Work-time Reduction and the Dutch Economic Miracle," (Toronto: 32 Hours: Action for Full Employment, 1999); Jelle Visser, "The first part-time economy in the world: a model to be followed?," *Journal of European Social Policy* 12, no. 1 (2002).

70 USDA, "Agricultural Fact Book, 2001-2002," ed. Office of Communications US Department of Agriculture (Washington D.C.: U.S. Government Printing Office, 2003); FAO, "The State of Food and Agriculture," (Rome: Food and Agricultural Organization of the United Nations, 2009).

71 Ibid.

72 P.W. Gerbens-Leenes and S. Nonhebel, "Consumption Patterns and their Effects on Land Required for Food," *Ecological Economics* 42(2002); Thomas White, "Diet and the Distribution of Environmental Impact," *Ecological Economics* 34(2000).

73 Booth, *The Coming Good Boom: Creating Prosperity for All and Saving the Environment through Compact Living.* Chapter 11.

74 Frank Newport, "In U.S., 5% Consider Themselves Vegetarians," Gallup Wellbeing, http://www.gallup.com/poll/156215/consider-themselves-vegetarians.aspx.

75 Thomas Dietz et al., "Values and Vegetarianism: An Exploratory Analysis," *Rural Sociology* 60(1995); Linda Kalof et al., "Social Psychology and Structural Influences on Vegetarian Beliefs," *Rural Sociology* 64(1999).

[76]Inglehart, "Public Support for Environmental Protection: Objective Problems and Subjective Values in 43 Societies."

[77]John Gelissen, "Explaining Popular Support for Environmental Protection: A Multilevel Analysis of 50 Nations," *Environment and Behavior* 39, no. 3 (2007).

[78]See the following references for the details behind the statistical results described here: Ibid.; A. Franzen and R. Meyer, "Environmental Attitudes in Cross-National Perspective: A Multilevel Analysis of the ISSP 1993 and 2000," *European Sociological Review* 26, no. 2 (2009); J. E. Givens and A. K. Jorgenson, "The Effects of Affluence, Economic Development, and Environmental Degradation on Environmental Concern: A Multilevel Analysis," *Organization & Environment* 24, no. 1 (2011); Raphael Nawrotzki, "The Politics of Environmental Concern: A Cross-National Analysis," *Organization & Environment* 25 (2012); Berit Kvaloy, Henning Finseraas, and Ola Listhaug, "The Publics' Concern for Global Warming: A Cross-National Study of 47 Countries," *Journal of Peace Research* 49(2012); Kvaloy, Finseraas, and Listhaug, "The Publics' Concern for Global Warming: A Cross-National Study of 47 Countries."; E. Tjernstrom and T. Tietenberg, "Do Differences in Attitudes Explain Differences in National Climate Change Policies?," *Ecological Economics* 65 (2012).

[79]Sammy Zahran et al., "Ecological Development and Global Climate Change: A Cross-National Study of Kyoto Protocol Ratification," *Society & Natural Resources* 20, no. 1 (2007).

[80]For the role of income in expressions of environmental concern, see Axel Franzen and Dominikus Vogl, "Acquiescence and the Willingness to Pay for Environmental Protection: A Comparison of the ISSP, WVS, and EVS," *Social Science Quarterly* 94, no. 3, (2012), 657-639; Jurgen Gerhards and Holger Lengfeld, "Support for European Union Environmental Policy by Citizens of EU-Member and Accession States," *Comparative Sociology* 7(2008).

[81]Gerhards and Lengfeld, "Support for European Union Environmental Policy by Citizens of EU-Member and Accession States."

[82]Kvaloy, Finseraas, and Listhaug, "The Publics' Concern for Global Warming: A Cross-National Study of 47 Countries."

[83]Tjernstrom and Tietenberg, "Do Differences in Attitudes Explain Differences in National Climate Change Policies?."

[84]Ibid.

[85]Douglas E. Booth, *Hooked on Growth: Economic Addictions and the Environment* (Lanham: Rowman & Littlefield, 2004). See Chapter 8.

[86]Booth, *The Coming Good Boom: Creating Prosperity for All and Saving the Environment through Compact Living.* Especially Chapters 8 and 9.

[87]Nuclear currently supplies 8 percent of total energy consumed in the U.S. See U.S. Energy Information Administration, "Annual Energy Review 2011," U.S. Energy Information Administration, www.eia.gov/totalenergy/data/annual/pdf/sec2.pdf.

[88]A 1% annual increase in output per capita over 40 years would mean a 50% increase in incomes on average.

[89]Max Wei, Shana Patadia, and Daniel M. Kammen, "Putting Renewables and Energy Efficiency to Work: How Many Jobs can the Clean Energy Industry Generate in the U.S.?," *Energy Policy* 38(2010).

[90]Ibid.

[91] Richard Rorty, *Philosophy and Social Hope* (New York: Penquin, 1999).

[92] Susmita Dasgupta et al., "The Impact of Sea Level Rise on Developing Countries: A Comparative Analysis," in *Working Paper 4136* (Washington D.C.: World Bank, 2007).

[93] Inglehart, "The Worldviews of Islamic Publics in Global Perspective."

[94] Kuhn, "On the Role of Human Development in the Arab Spring."

[95] Mark Tessler, "Do Islamic Orientations Influence Attitudes toward Democracy in the Arab World? Evidence from the World Values Survey in Egypt, Jordan, Morocco, and Algeria," in *Values and Perceptions of the Islamic and Middle Eastern Publics*, ed. Mansoor Moaddel (New York: Palgrave, 2007).

[96] Welzel and Inglehart, "The Role of Ordinary People in Democratization."

[97] Gillian Rice, "Pro-environmental Behavior in Egypt: Is there a Role for Islamic Environmental Ethics?," *Journal of Business Ethics* 65, no. 4 (2006).

[98] Brigitte Hoogendoorn and Chantal Hartog, "Prevalence and Determinants of Social Entrepreneurshp at the Macro-level," in *EIM Research Reports* (Zoetermeer: Panteia/ EIM, 2011).

200

99   Lorraine Uhlaner and Roy Thurik, "Postmaterialism influencing total entrepreneurial activity across nations," *Journal of Evolutionary Economics* 17, no. 2 (2007).

100 Ibrahim Abouleish and Helmy Abouleish, "Garden in the Desert: Sekem Makes Comprehensive Sustainable Development a Reality " *Innovations* 3(2008); Ibrahim Abouleish, *Sekem: A Sustainable Community in the Egyptian Desert* (Edinburgh: Floris Books, 2005).

101 Abouleish and Abouleish, "Garden in the Desert: Sekem Makes Comprehensive Sustainable Development a Reality ".

102   Yusif Genc, Julie Hayes, and Yuri Shavrukov, "Hydroponics - A Standard Methodology for Plant Biological Researches," ResearchGate, http://www.researchgate.net/publication/233927805_Hydroponics_-_A_Standard_Methodology_for_Plant_Biological_Researc hes?ev=pub_srch_pub.

103 Megan Detrie, "'Schaduf' sets up rooftop urban farms for low-income families," *Egypt Independent*, March 16, 2012.

104 DESERTEC Foundation, "Clean Power from Deserts: The DESERTEC Concept for Energy, Water and Climate Security," in *WhiteBook* (Bonn: DESERTEC Foundation, 2009); World Bank, "Middle East and North Africa Region Assessment of Local Manufacturing Potential for Concentrating Solar Power (CSP) Projects," (Washington D.C.: World Bank, 2011).

105 The price has dropped recently to around 3 Euros because of the current economic crisis but will rise in the future as the economy recovers and emission caps are tightened.

[106] DESERTEC Foundation, "DESERTEC Milestones," http://www.desertec.org/global-mission/milestones/.

[107] DESERTEC Foundation, "Clean Power from Deserts: The DESERTEC Concept for Energy, Water and Climate Security," in *WhiteBook* (Bonn: DESERTEC Foundation, 2009).

[108] Booth, *The Coming Good Boom: Creating Prosperity for All and Saving the Environment through Compact Living*. See pages 65-66.

[109] Bernard Yaros, "Solar Power Initiative Could Make Egypt Power Source for Europe," *Tunisia LIve*, February 8 2012; TuNur, "TuNur Project," TuNur Project, http:// www.tunur.tn/.

[110] Justin Shilad, "Can Local and Regional Projects Help Renewable Energy go Mainstream?," *Egypt Independent*, December 12, 2012.

[111] Steven Viney, "KarmSolar Develops Renewable Energy Solution for 'Off Grid' Farmers," *Egypt Indepedent*, March 22, 2012.

[112] H.K. Soussa, "Effects of Drip Irrigation Water Amount on Crop Yield, Productivity and Efficiency of Water Use in Desert Regions in Egypt," *Nile Basin Water Science & Engineering Journal* 3(2010); Mona Mourshed, "Rethinking Irrigation Technology Adoption: Lessons from the Egyptian Desert," in *Working Paper Number 23, Program in Science, Technology, and Society* (Cambridge: MIT, 1995).

[113] Louise Sarant, "Renewable Energy Forum at the Arab League: On Regulations and Pan-Arabism," *Egypt Independent*, April 24, 2012.

[114] Chiara Trabacchi, Valerio Micale, and Gianleo Frisari, "San Giorgio Group Case Study: Prosol Tunisia," (San Francisco: Climate Policy Initiaitve, 2012); Samantha Olz and Lawrence Agbemabiese, "Innovative Energy Policy in a Developing Country Context: Experience from UNEP's PROSOL Initiative," *Wiley Interdisciplinary Reviews: Energy and Environment* 1(2012); Myriem Touhami and Ghita Hannane, "PROSOL: Financing Solar Water Heating in Tunisia," United Nations Environment Programme, DTIE, http://climatepolicyinitiative.org/wp-content/uploads/2011/12/Touhami-and-Hannane_PROSOL.pdf.

[115] David Sims, *Understanding Cairo: The Logic of a City Out of Control* (Cairo: American University in Cairo Press, 2010).

[116] Anne Nicole Duquennois and Peter Newman, "Linking the Green and Brown Agendas: A Case Study on Cairo, Egypt," in *Revisiting Urban Planning: Global Report on Human Settlements 2009* (2009).

[117] J.R. Kenworthy, "Transport Energy Use and Greenhouse Gases in Urban Passenger Transport Systems: A Study of 84 Global Cities," (Murdoch, Western Australia: Murdoch University, 2003).

[118] Duquennois and Newman, "Linking the Green and Brown Agendas: A Case Study on Cairo, Egypt."

[119] Manal El-Batran and Christian Arandel, "A Shelter of their Own: Informal Settlement Expansion in Greater Cairo and Government Responses," *Environment and Urbanization* 10(1998).Sims, *Understanding Cairo: The Logic of a City Out of Control.* My discussion of Cairo's development here owes much to Sims.

[120] Kuhn, "On the Role of Human Development in the Arab Spring."; United Nations Human Development Program (UNDP), "International Human Development Indicators," UNDP, http://hdr.undp.org/en/statistics/data/.

[121] Welzel and Inglehart, "The Role of Ordinary People in Democratization."

[122] Inglehart, "The Worldviews of Islamic Publics in Global Perspective."

[123] Duquennois and Newman, "Linking the Green and Brown Agendas: A Case Study on Cairo, Egypt."; Sims, *Understanding Cairo: The Logic of a City Out of Control.* See Chapter 8 in Sims.

[124] Ronald Albers and Marga Peeters, "Food and Energy Prices, Government Subsidies and Fiscal Balances in South Mediterranean Countries," in *Economics Paper 437* (Brussels2011).

[125] Duquennois and Newman, "Linking the Green and Brown Agendas: A Case Study on Cairo, Egypt."

[126] Robert D. Putnam and David E. Campbell, *American Grace: How Religion Divides and Unites Us* (New York: Simon & Schuster, 2010).

[127] Nietzsche, *Thus Spoke Zarathustra: A Book for None and All.* 13.

[128] Ibid. 15.

[129] Ibid. 36.

[130] Ibid. 122.

[131] Ibid. 73-74.

[132] Martin Heidegger, "What Are Poets For?," in *Poetry, Language, Thought* (New York: Harper & Row, 2001). 97.

[133] Ibid. 107-108.

[134] Ibid. 123.

[135] Heidegger, "The Thing." 166.

204

[136] Ibid. 169-170.

[137] Ibid.

[138] Putnam and Campbell, *American Grace: How Religion Divides and Unites Us*.

[139] Houtman and Aupers, "The Spiritual Turn and the Decline of Tradition: The Spread of Post-Christian Spirituality in 14 Western Countries, 1981–2000."; Siobhan Chandler, "The Social Ethic of Religiously Unaffiliated Spirituality," *Religious Compass* 2(2008).

[140] Hagevi, "Beyond Church and State: Private Religiosity and Post-Materialist Political Opinion among Individuals in Sweden."; Houtman and Aupers, "The Spiritual Turn and the Decline of Tradition: The Spread of Post-Christian Spirituality in 14 Western Countries, 1981–2000."

[141] Ibid.

[142] Botvar, "Alternative Religion – A New Political Cleavage?: An Analysis of Norwegian Survey Data on New Forms of Spirituality."

[143] Jon P. Bloch, "Alternative Spirituality and Environmentalism," *Review of Religion Research* 40 (1998).

[144] James L. Guth et al., "Faith and the Environment: Religious Beliefs and Attitudes on Environmental Policy," *American Journal of Political Science* 39(1995).

[145] David Worth, "Our New Cathedrals: Spirituality and Old-Growth Forests in Western Australia," *Portal Journal of Multidisciplinary Studies* 3(2006), http://epress.lib.uts.edu.au/journals/index.php/portal/article/view/124.

[146] Aldo Leopold, *A Sand County Almanac: With Essays on Conservation from Round River* (New York: Ballantine Books, 1970).

[147] Heidegger, "The Question Concerning Technology."

Index

210